The Leadership Partnership

The Leadership Partnership

Second Edition

DARYL FISCHER AND LAURA B. ROBERTS

ROWMAN & LITTLEFIELD
Lanham • Boulder • New York • London

Published by Rowman & Littlefield
A wholly owned subsidary of The Rowman & Littlefield Publishing Group, Inc.
4501 Forbes Boulevard, Suite 200, Lanham, Maryland 20706
www.rowman.com

Unit A, Whitacre Mews, 26-34 Stannary Street, London SE11 4AB

British Library Cataloguing in Publication Information Available

Library of Congress Cataloging-in-Publication Data Available

ISBN: 9781538108413 (pbk. : alk. paper)
ISBN: 9781538108420 (electronic)

♾️™ The paper used in this publication meets the minimum requirements of American National Standard for Information Sciences—Permanence of Paper for Printed Library Materials, ANSI/NISO Z39.48-1992.

Printed in the United States of America

Contents

Foreword

Thank you for your purchase of *The Leadership Partnership*. Since its founding, the Museum Trustee Association (MTA) has communicated strategies and best practices to museums across the Americas. We are especially proud of this latest edition of our *Templates for Trustees* series, which digs deeper into trusteeship than ever before and provides the tools for an institution of any size to build, educate, and inspire a successful board.

Throughout the following pages are guidelines and best practices from industry leaders, both staff and volunteers. You will also find five customizable and automated templates to help you keep your board organized and focused on the key issues and challenges facing your museum today. MTA staff is available to you for support as you work your way through the software.

MTA is the network for informing, advising, and inspiring museum trustees. For more information on our products, publications, and services, visit us at www.museumtrustee.org or call our offices. We look forward to hearing from you!

Richard Kelly
Board Chairman
Museum Trustee Association

Mary Baily Wieler
President
Museum Trustee Association

About *Templates for Trustees*

"When it comes to board information," says Harvard University professor Richard Chait, "less is more, and much less is much more."[1] Trustees usually receive too much information with too little meaning. Instead, they need structured, concise materials that enhance board performance and satisfaction while directing their attention to what matters most.

Templates for Trustees is a four-part series designed by the Museum Trustee Association (MTA) to focus attention on key processes and tasks of governance. It supports the MTA's mission "to enhance the effectiveness of museum trustees" by

- promoting and facilitating dialogue between museum trustees and museum directors
- collecting and disseminating information on museum governance that will assist trustees in discharging their responsibilities more effectively
- providing education and training opportunities for museum trustees
- initiating and conducting research on issues of concern to museum trustees

The templates are tools that present board information so that it can be collected, explored, and understood from different perspectives. Each one helps boards create documents, spreadsheets, and presentations tailored to their own needs. Using fill-in-the-blank forms, surveys, and rating scales that are provided on a unique cloud-based app, trustees or administrators enter specific information about their museum and their board. The completed templates and reports serve as starting points to help boards organize their thoughts, identify their priorities, and plan their actions.

The Leadership Partnership is the second volume in the series. Other volumes include: *Building Museum Boards* (volume 1), *Executive Transitions* (volume 3), and *Strategic Thinking and Planning* (volume 4). All books in the series are available on a web-based application that is accessible to both PC and Mac users.

All four volumes have five sections:

- **Using the *Templates for Trustees* Online App** provides an overview of how the website is structured and a brief description of the purpose and functionality of each template and report. Specific instructions for working with the document library and web-based forms and customizing the templates for each museum's needs are available on the website. This online **Help Manual** will be useful to the administrator—the staff or the board member who will modify the forms so they are tailored to individual boards.

- The **User's Guide** suggests how to take full advantage of the text, templates, resources, and appendices. It also provides a brief overview of the entire assessment process, which will be useful to the administrator and everyone on the Governance Committee or ad hoc task force responsible for assessment.
- An introduction that provides a summary of relevant issues and trends, **The Importance of Partnerships and Assessment**, sets the stage for the work.
- **Chapters 1–4** discuss the templates more fully and present examples of filled-in templates from a hypothetical board.
- The **Resource Guide** includes publications and organizations with additional information on board leadership and assessment.

TERMINOLOGY

In these volumes we have used the following terms:

- *Template library* includes the complete set of tools: surveys, database forms, documents, calendars, and presentations.
- *Template* refers to any tool that is modified by the administrator and filled out by board members.
- *Reports* are generated by compiling the responses to completed templates.
- *Trustee* refers to a member of the museum's governing board. We use the terms *board member* and *trustee* interchangeably throughout this manual.
- *Director* is the staff leader who reports to the board. Some museums may use *executive director, chief executive officer (CEO),* or *president.*
- *Board chair* is the senior board member who oversees all board functions. Some boards may use *chief volunteer officer (CVO)* or *president.*
- *Administrator* is the individual—typically a staff member in the executive office—who facilitates the search process and modifies and manages the templates.
- *Governance Committee* is the standing committee charged with generating and maintaining a healthy board. It may also be referred to as the *Nominating Committee,* the *Board Development Committee,* or the *Governance and Board Development Committee.*

TEMPLATE SUPPORT

The Museum Trustee Association provides support to boards that purchase *Templates for Trustees.* Please contact the MTA at Support@MuseumTrusteeTemplates.org

- for more information or to order additional volumes in the series
- with questions about tailoring or troubleshooting your templates (service included in the one-time setup fee)
- if you would like to make a testimonial about your experience using this or other volumes in the *Templates for Trustees* series

NOTE

1. Chait made this observation during a panel on "The New Work of the Nonprofit Board" at the American Association of Museums Annual Meeting in Baltimore, Maryland, April 2000.

Using the *Templates for Trustees* Online App

The physical book you are holding in your hands is just one part of *The Leadership Partnership*. The templates themselves, which can be tailored to your institution, are stored in an online application hosted by the Museum Trustee Association (MTA). To activate your account in the application, you will need to contact the MTA at support@museumtrusteetemplates.org, pay a modest one-time setup fee (waived for MTA members), and schedule a time to set up your account. Once you create an account, you can begin to review and customize the five templates in *The Leadership Partnership*.

Throughout *The Leadership Partnership* and the other books in the series, there is an important role for the "administrator" who manages the museum's use of the online application. In a larger museum, there may be someone who already manages board communication as part of his or her job. In a smaller museum, the administrator may be the director or a board member. It is also possible for two people to share that role. Once you have identified the individual who will fill that role, he or she should set up the application.

INITIAL SETUP

Step one is registering your account with the Museum Trustee Association by sending an email to support@ museumtrusteetemplates.org. The MTA staff member responsible for administering *Templates for Trustees* will send the administrator a short version of your museum's name (Museum ID), the administrator's username, and a password, which will ensure the privacy and security of your museum's information. MTA staff will also schedule a telephone call to go through the rest of the setup process.

Step two is logging into the application at www.museumtrusteetemplates.org. The first screen (figure 0.1) is the *Templates for Trustees* landing page, with general information about the MTA.

From there, click "Log in" on the blue bar to continue. Enter the information provided by MTA (figure 0.2).

After logging in, you will be on the landing page for the four volumes in *Templates for Trustees* (figure 0.3).

Step three: Before setting up any single volume, the administrator should establish the global settings. This will enable the application to customize the templates (figure 0.4). Click on "Settings" to launch the page with the placeholder settings. For each item in Settings—the museum name, mission statement, director's name, the title used by the director, and the first month of the museum's fiscal year, annual meeting, or the start of the board cycle—click on "Edit" and put the appropriate information in the field labeled "Setting Value." Click "Save," and you will be returned to the list of Settings. *Note*: You will not see the changes immediately. Close this menu. Reopen "Settings," and you will see the changes.

For the Settings menu and most of the screenshots that follow, the information is for a fictitious museum—the Greenville Museum of Art and History—and its board.

FIGURE 0.1
MTA *Templates for Trustees* Home Page (Courtesy of the Museum Trustee Association)

FIGURE 0.2
MTA *Templates for Trustees* Log In (Courtesy of the Museum Trustee Association)

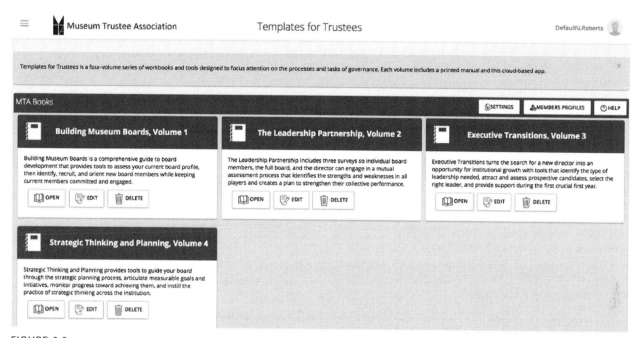

FIGURE 0.3
MTA *Templates for Trustees* Four Volumes Landing Page (Courtesy of the Museum Trustee Association)

Step four is creating a *Templates for Trustees* user account for everyone currently on the board, the director, and the administrator. Next to the MTA logo is a three-bar icon that opens the "Administration" menu (figure 0.5). Click that, and a new column will open on the left side with an arrow next to "Administration" (figure 0.6). Click on the arrow to open the menu and select "Users" (figure 0.7).

Click on the blue "Create New User" box (figure 0.8).

Settings/Placeholders

Description	Value		
The title used by the director	Executive Director	EDIT	DELETE
The director's name	Jordan Charles	EDIT	DELETE
The museum's mission statement	Greenville Museum of Art and History broadens and deepens the community's connections to the heritage and culture of the region.	EDIT	DELETE
Month of the annual meeting and board elections	January	EDIT	DELETE
The name of the museum	Greenville Museum of Art and History	EDIT	DELETE

CLOSE

FIGURE 0.4
MTA *Templates for Trustees* Global Settings (Courtesy of the Museum Trustee Association)

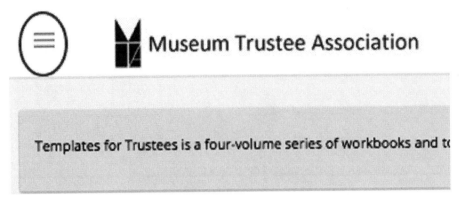

FIGURE 0.5
The Leadership Partnership Administration Menu Opener (Courtesy of the Museum Trustee Association)

A window will pop up (figure 0.9) where you can enter basic information for each member of the board: name, email address, and a username. We suggest deciding on a convention for creating usernames: *first initial last name* is common. Note that the system will automatically send the new user an email with instructions for choosing a personal password.

Every user has one or more "roles" that determine their access to various features. In general, the roles are members and chair of the relevant committee (for this template, the Assessment Task Force), board members, Executive Committee members, board chair, executive director, and administrator. Just above the user's name, you will see "Roles" and a number in a blue circle. At first, that number will be "1" for the basic role of User. To add roles, click that circle. A menu of further roles opens; check all roles that user has and save (figure 0.10).

Because each of the roles will have different needs for information, there are different levels of access to templates and reports. Aside from the administrator, the chair of the Assessment Task Force will have the most extensive access to the files in this volume. Members of the Assessment Task Force will have greater access than

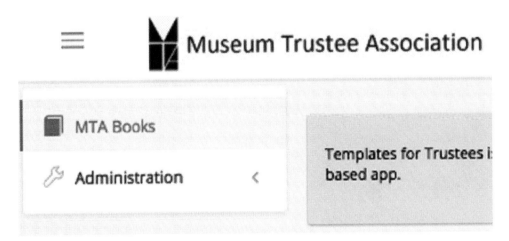

FIGURE 0.6
The Leadership Partnership Administration Menu Selections (Courtesy of the Museum Trustee Association)

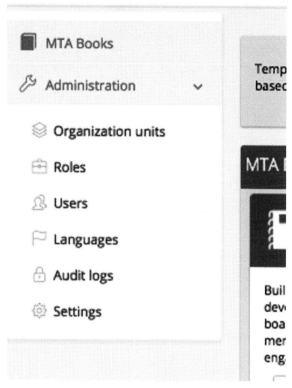

FIGURE 0.7

The Leadership Partnership Administration Menu Selector (Courtesy of the Museum Trustee Association)

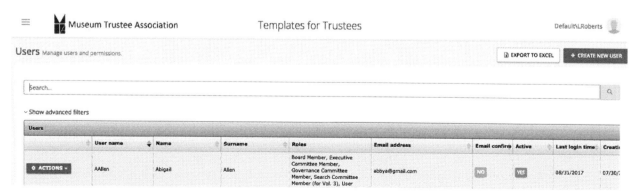

FIGURE 0.8

The Leadership Partnership New User Setup (Courtesy of the Museum Trustee Association)

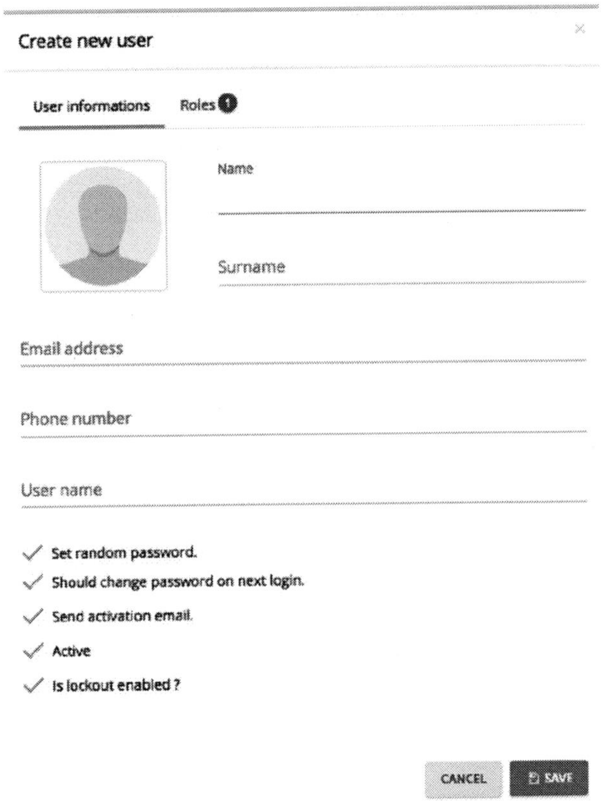

Create new user   ×

User informations   **Roles** ❶

| | Name |
| | Surname |

Email address

Phone number

User name

✓ Set random password.
✓ Should change password on next login.
✓ Send activation email.
✓ Active
✓ Is lockout enabled ?

CANCEL   🖫 SAVE

FIGURE 0.9
The Leadership Partnership New User Activation (Courtesy of the Museum Trustee Association)

Create new user   ×

User informations   **Roles** ❶

☐ Administrator
☐ Assessment Task Force Chair (for Vol. 2)
☐ Assessment Task Force Member (for Vol. 2)
☐ Board Administrator
☐ Board Chair
☐ Board Member
☐ Director
☐ Executive Committee Member
☐ Governance Committee Chair
☐ Governance Committee Member
☐ Search Committee Chair (for Vol. 3)
☐ Search Committee Member (for Vol. 3)
☐ Strategic Planning Committee Chair (for Vol. 4)
☐ Strategic Planning Committee Member (for Vol. 4)
✓ User

CANCEL   🖫 SAVE

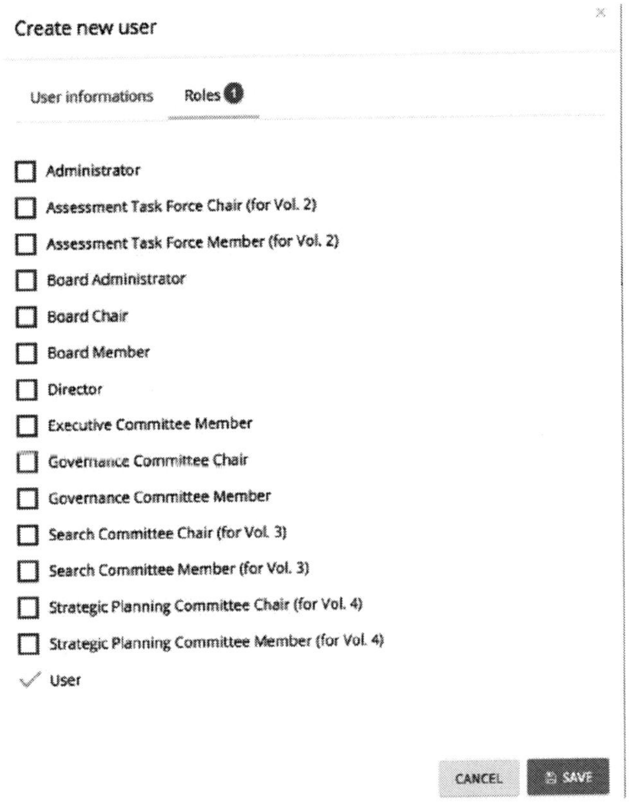

FIGURE 0.10
The Leadership Partnership User Roles (Courtesy of the Museum Trustee Association)

FIGURE 0.11

The Leadership Partnership User Edits (Courtesy of the Museum Trustee Association)

other members of the board so that they can do the work of the task force. (Please note: Because this list of users is accessed by all of the *Templates for Trustees*, there are roles that are not relevant to *The Leadership Partnership*. The administrator can add those roles when setting up other volumes.)

All of the users are entered into a table for further customizing and editing (figure 0.11). Click the blue "Actions" button next to the user's name and select "Edit." There is also a button that allows the administrator to "Create New User," which brings up the same screen shown in figure 0.9.

Every user must have an email address associated with their user profile. If one or more board members do not use email, we suggest setting up an account on the museum's email system, with mail forwarded to the administrator. That way, whenever an email is generated for the board member(s), the administrator will receive the intended survey, report, form, or document and can print a hard copy to send to the board member(s) by mail or arrange for it to be picked up at the museum.

Step five: Having set up all of the museum's users, it is time to start using the templates. Return to the three-bar menu next to the MTA logo and select "MTA Books" (figure 0.12), which will bring you back to the landing page

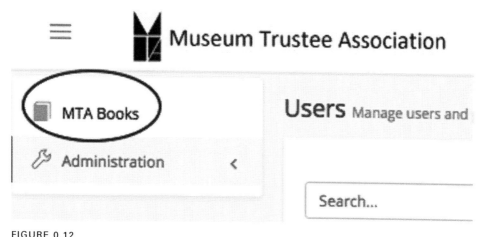

FIGURE 0.12

MTA *Templates for Trustees* Four Volumes Landing Page (Courtesy of the Museum Trustee Association)

FIGURE 0.13
Templates for Trustees Help Button (Courtesy of the Museum Trustee Association)

for the four volumes in *Templates for Trustees*. Having purchased *The Leadership Partnership*, that publication will be live.

In addition to these basic instructions, *Templates for Trustees* has an online Help function with more detailed and specific instructions. The "Help" button is always on the blue bar, next to "Settings" and "Members Profiles" (figure 0.13).

The Leadership Partnership User's Guide

Board assessment plays a critical part in organizational learning. It challenges board members and directors to look at things analytically so that all aspects of leadership are taken into the mix; systematically so that even long-established traditions and familiar patterns are examined; broadly so that all perspectives are considered; and regularly so that assessment is seen as a normal part of the leadership—and the learning—routine.

A board undertaking the assessments in *The Leadership Partnership* should assign responsibility for managing the process to a standing committee or ad hoc task force. For many boards, the Executive Committee (comprising the officers and other board leadership) would be the logical group, particularly if it is responsible for the annual review of the director. By contrast, the Governance Committee is generally charged with improving board performance and the Personnel Committee with staff performance. This could be an excellent project for an ad hoc task force with members from all three committees and perhaps some additional members-at-large.

The Leadership Partnership includes five online templates. The first four are designed to help trustees and directors identify their individual strengths and challenges. The fifth template (a slide presentation) will help them focus on improving their collective performance.

Template 1: Individual Board Member Activity gathers data—primarily hard numbers—about the participation and contributions of each board member as a reference for the committee or task force charged with this assessment.

Template 2: Self-Assessment examines softer but equally valuable data about individual board members' attitudes, participation, and contributions. It includes both a questionnaire and open-ended questions to gather information from individual board members about their attitudes and expectations, serving as a means of personal reflection and a reference for the Governance Committee or task force. The online app tabulates and summarizes data in reports and graphs.

Template 3: Board Assessment examines the board's collective performance from the perspectives of trustees and the director. Completed annually, the template includes a questionnaire and open-ended questions about board performance to be completed by each trustee and the director. Because this data is gathered annually, we suggest saving the reports and comparing them from year to year to track changes and monitor progress.

Template 4: Director Assessment is analogous to the Board Assessment, examining the director's performance from the perspectives of the board and the director. This template includes a questionnaire about the director's performance to be completed by each trustee and the director.

Template 5: The Leadership Plan is a presentation to help identify areas of strength and weakness, agreement and disagreement, and to develop a plan that balances and strengthens the leadership partnership. Designed to spark and guide a dialogue between the board and the director, the presentation includes nineteen slides that the administrator can tailor to what is revealed in the previous templates.

Templates 2, 3, and 4 generate a series of reports that can readily be viewed online. The data in the reports can also be downloaded as spreadsheets. Someone with good facility in formatting spreadsheets can then prepare documents to share with the committee or task force responsible for assessment.

These assessment tools challenge trustees and directors to view their performance from multiple perspectives. Each arm of governance has different and valuable viewpoints that can inform the other, contributing to a broader picture of the partnership and leading to more effective performance for everyone. It's not enough for trustees to evaluate themselves by looking around the board table. The director needs to share what he or she sees of the board from the executive office. In the same way, the board cannot assess the director's performance without factoring his or her perspective into the assessment equation. The statements in Templates 2, 3, and 4 fall into ten parallel categories (shown in table 0.1). The specific statements reflect distinctions between the roles of individual members, the board as a whole, and the director. All three assessments can be administered at the same time or in sequence over several weeks or months.

Table 0.1. Assessment Categories

	Self-Assessment	*Board Assessment*	*Director Assessment*
I. Big Picture	Mission, Vision, and Strategy	Mission, Vision, and Strategy	Mission, Vision, and Strategy
II. Development	Personal Development	Board Membership and Development	Staff and Board Development
III. Operations	Board Participation	Board Operations	Board Meetings
IV. Board Relationships	Individual-Board Relationship	Board-Director Partnership	Director-Board Partnership
V. Staff Relationships	Individual-Staff Relationship	Board-Staff Relationship	Staff Management
VI. Oversight	Individual Oversight	Board Oversight	Director Oversight
VII. Finances	Financial Oversight and Contributions	Financial Stewardship and Fundraising	Financial Planning and Resource Development
VIII. Collections	Collections Knowledge	Collections Stewardship	Collections Management
IX. Facilities	Facilities	Facilities Management	Facilities Management
X. External Relations	Museum Advocate	Community Engagement	Public Engagement

INTERPRETING OPEN-ENDED QUESTIONS

All three templates end with a few open-ended questions. These questions contribute to a deeper, more nuanced understanding of the leadership partnership. Although the online app will collect and report all of the answers, it will not analyze the responses to open-ended questions. If you have a board member with experience in market research or program assessment, ask that person to help analyze responses to the open-ended questions. If not, try one of the following approaches:

- Ask one or two members of the committee or task force administering *The Leadership Partnership* to sort responses to the open-ended questions into like groups and identify each with a short phrase or heading.
- At a meeting of the committee, ask each member to review all the responses and choose the one they find most relevant to the strong functioning of the board and director and the one that's most relevant to board satisfaction. Write each on a separate Post-it note, and arrange them in clusters on a flip chart to identify areas of affinity.
- Create word clouds from responses using one of the many apps that are readily available online.

A HYPOTHETICAL BOARD

Because the reports are empty until data is entered, survey results for a hypothetical board of twelve people have been entered to create reports for Templates 2, 3, and 4. For each of these templates, **Survey Responses by Ques-**

tion reports the distribution of responses by question and category. **Survey Responses by Member** reports the scores for each of the twelve members (recorded anonymously). There is an additional report for Templates 3 and 4, **Survey Responses by Group**, which identifies the five members of the Executive Committee and reports the average scores for that group, the board members-at-large, and the entire board; the differences in perspective among them may be significant. This report also separates the responses of the director and compares them to the overall board averages.

Acknowledgments

John Adkins's thirty years of experience with technology includes writing apps for Fortune 500 companies. His knowledge and experience helped move *Templates for Trustees* into the twenty-first century with the introduction of the online app that is an integral part of each volume in this series. We are grateful for his creativity and persistence, which met every challenge we encountered in implementing this new platform.

The Museum Trustee Association and the authors thank Barbara Booker, coauthor of the first edition, and the dedicated group of advisors who contributed to that publication. We also thank David Ellis for his wise advice and counsel on museum leadership in the writing of this new edition.

The Institute of Museum and Library Services, the primary source of federal support for the nation's museums and libraries, helped make possible the publication of the first edition of *The Leadership Partnership*.

The Museum Trustee Association gratefully acknowledges the following donors whose support made this series possible:

The Wieler Family Foundation in honor of Mary Baily Wieler and Emily Inglis
Georgina T. and Thomas A. Russo
Margaret and Bill Benjamin
Andrew L. and Gayle Shaw Camden
Richard and Mary Kelly
Maureen Pecht King
Janis and William Wetsman Foundation
Kristine and Leland Peterson
Katherine Duff Rines

Introduction

The Importance of Partnerships and Assessment

LEADERSHIP IS A PARTNERSHIP

Leadership is a partnership, not a solo performance. The best director can't lead alone, and neither can the strongest board chair. The responsibility for governing and guiding a museum is shared among the board of trustees and the director. Each has a distinct but complementary set of responsibilities, which together provide the basis for strategic thinking, policymaking, and management. In an ideal situation, both partners—the board and the director—are strong and vital, carrying their full weight of responsibility. In the reality of most institutions, each has strong points and weak spots. Identifying these makes it easier for trustees and directors to capitalize on each other's strengths and compensate for each other's weaknesses.

As nonprofit management becomes more challenging, thinking about the relationship between the board and the director is evolving. The bright line between the board's responsibility for policy and the staff's responsibility for management is blurring. Writing in *Nonprofit Quarterly* in 2006, Mary Hiland cited a 2005 study of eighteen pairs of board chairs and executive directors from nonprofit organizations located in Silicon Valley, California. Trust, rather than clearly delineated roles, was cited as the single most important dynamic influencing behavior and performance. Len Shuster, board chair of the Computer History Museum and quoted in the article, observed, "It's much more complicated than it would seem if you read the books that say, 'This is the role of the executive director and this is the role of the chairman.' In any real organization . . . it depends a lot on the reasonableness of the people involved to make it work. If you try to just play by the rules, it's not going to work." Hiland went on to observe, "The process of give and take, working it out together, was characteristic of the strongest partnerships. Reliance on structure (i.e., prescriptive roles) was evident only in low-trust relationships."[1]

The report *Museum Board Leadership 2017*, produced by BoardSource for the American Alliance of Museums, presents interesting but nuanced findings. On the positive side, "59% of museum directors give their board chair an A grade for cultivating a productive, constructive partnership with the museum director" and "51% . . . rank their board chairs as their #1 go-to person when they have a need to consult frankly on a tough decision." The findings are less encouraging when it comes to the board as a whole. Both museum directors and board chairs give their boards grades of B on "Guiding and supporting the director," B– on "Understanding roles and responsibilities," and B– or C+ on "Evaluating the director."[2] Obviously, there is room for improvement.

There is clearly a need for greater communication and work with the board around fundraising. Museums are more likely to engage in fundraising than other nonprofits (94 percent versus 86 percent of all nonprofits) but in the survey "only 39% of museum directors agree or strongly agree that their board actively participates in fundraising versus relying mostly on the director and staff." *Museum Board Leadership 2017* goes on to note that "only 54% of museums set the stage for fundraising early on by explaining expectations during the recruitment process. . . .

Given the proper orientation and training, any board member who is willing to learn can become a highly valuable and effective member of the fundraising team."[3] The assessment questions about Development and Finances can be an excellent starting point for initiating these conversations.

ASSESSMENT BENEFITS ALL

Many museum trustees approach assessment with fear and trepidation, which may date back to their memories of taking tests in school. Decades later, they may still be uncomfortable with pressure to perform according to someone else's standards. The idea of being evaluated may be especially unappealing to individuals who generously volunteer their time and share their resources. But once the benefits are realized, the process actually builds confidence in individuals and in the institutions they lead. While the board and director have much to gain, the benefits of regular, mutual assessment extend far beyond the leadership circle.

- For the **board**, clearly articulated criteria and accurate, easily understandable data help everyone come together to focus on shared assumptions about the organization's goals and priorities.
- For the **director**, assessment that is based on objective criteria rather than subjective opinion provides a firm footing for management. Knowing where he or she stands makes it is easier for the director to lead staff and volunteers.
- For the **staff**, assessment of the board and the director creates clearer goals for staff performance and clearer criteria for measuring the effectiveness of exhibitions and programs. Staff and volunteer morale will increase when the director and the board model effective assessment.
- For the **community**, assessment of the board and director gives the museum's constituency increasing confidence in its leadership.
- For **funders**—government agencies, private foundations, corporations, or individuals—assessment demonstrates that the board is self-reflective. Funders especially appreciate assessment that notes areas of improvement in museum leadership.

WHAT IS EFFECTIVE ASSESSMENT?

To maximize the effectiveness of *The Leadership Partnership*, everyone involved in the assessment process should subscribe to certain values. Effective assessment is:

- **comprehensive**, providing a full picture of the leadership partnership and the governance process
- **analytical**, examining individual aspects of board and director roles
- **objective**, helping both arms of governance to look at their performance without bias
- **systemic**, focusing on the entire organization rather than on individuals or personalities
- **mutually beneficial**, helping trustees and directors to perform better with input from one another
- **measurable**, making the criteria for assessment as clear as possible to all parties
- **specific**, focusing on leadership in museums rather than nonprofits in general
- **regular**, becoming a routine part of the governance process
- **proactive** rather than reactive, making assessment most productive when the museum is not facing a major problem or crisis
- **provocative**, inspiring dialogue and getting people to think in new ways

THE TOUCHSTONE FOR ASSESSMENT

Mission is the touchstone for all board, staff, and volunteer activities, and it must be kept in mind in all types of individual and institutional assessment. The American Alliance of Museums identifies the mission statement as one of five "core documents" that demonstrate a museum's commitment to professional standards and practices.

> All museums are expected to have a formally stated and approved mission that states what the museum does, for whom and why. A museum's mission statement is the primary benchmark against which to evaluate the museum's performance. One of the two core questions underlying any assessment of compliance with national standards is: How well does the museum achieve its stated mission and goals? This emphasis acknowledges an effective and replicable practice: Museums that use clearly delineated mission statements to guide their activities and decisions are more likely to function effectively.[4]

To remind board members and the director of the reason for their efforts and to help them measure their effectiveness, these templates keep the museum's mission statement front and center.

LIVING, LEARNING BOARDS

Boards are dynamic, living organisms, ever growing and constantly changing. As such, they are best understood when viewed over an extended period. A single assessment is like a snapshot; it captures a picture of the leadership partnership at a particular moment. The board and director can step back and ask, "How can we get ourselves in a little better shape? How do we want to look the next time someone snaps a picture?"

It helps to remember that we all look different at different times in our lives. That's why it's important for museum leaders to monitor the effectiveness of their partnership over several years. These surveys should be administered annually and results compared from year to year. After gathering enough data to suggest a trend, executive and board leaders should ask, "Is this a pattern we want to continue or one we want to reverse?" In board dynamics, as in physics, inertia is a powerful force. If the leadership partnership is strong and healthy, chances are good that it will continue to grow and flourish. If the partnership is weak, chances are that it will continue to falter until the critical issues are identified and the necessary changes made.

Effective assessment is not an occasional activity separate from board governance but a regular and integral part of museum leadership. It inspires reflection, which helps boards and directors become aware of the *how* as well as the *what* of leadership. Reflecting on executive and board decisions will bring continual improvement in the decision-making process. Reflecting on board meetings will help museum leaders make better use of their time together. Reflecting on board composition and structure will build boards that can advance their museums' strategic priorities.

To make assessment a habit and get your board in shape, Richard Chait recommends that boards conduct mini-evaluations at the conclusion of each meeting by asking members to rate the performance of the board on a 1–5 scale.[5] The questions should be simple, such as the following:

- The issues covered today were . . . (trivial to essential)
- The materials provided were . . . (worthless to invaluable)
- Today's topics were primarily . . . (operational to strategic)
- The majority of time was spent . . . (listening to reports to engaging in dialogue)

The survey might include one or two open-ended questions such as

- What was the most valuable thing we accomplished at today's meeting?
- Is there a question that was not adequately answered in today's meeting?

With opportunities to provide regular feedback, trustees and directors alike will grow more comfortable evaluating and discussing their own performance. Once boards get in the habit of reflecting on what they're doing and how they're doing it, they'll see that assessment is one of the most valuable of all governance routines. Weighing accomplishments and measuring progress against goals is a way of thinking and acting strategically. It is something that effective leaders do instinctively and everyone can learn to do with practice.

In addition to regular self-assessment, it's important for boards to solicit the opinion of objective outsiders. Every few years it's a good idea to seek help from a consultant, a director of another museum, or a member of another nonprofit board. Moving beyond the realm of self-perception to incorporate the perspectives of others with governance experience will help museum leaders see their own institutions in new ways and consider new approaches to familiar challenges.

Outside facilitators can help in several ways. They can keep discussions open and focused on the issues. They can bring a fresh perspective and see beyond individual differences that sometimes divide members of the board. Outsiders may also be able to uncover "invisible" issues that are so much a part of the institutional culture that they won't surface in an internal assessment or discussion. After reviewing the results of the board and director assessments, some boards may wish to ask an outside facilitator to lead a discussion at a special meeting or board retreat. In addition to consultants who specialize in meeting facilitation, there are probably skilled staff at organizations and companies in your community who might be available pro bono. You might also consider an experienced member of another board. If there is a wide disparity in responses on certain issues, an outside facilitator might be helpful in bridging the gaps. Or, if there is strong consensus about problems with leadership, a facilitator might suggest new approaches that may not come out of internal discussions.

EXIT INTERVIEWS
Don't miss opportunities to get feedback from board members who retire or resign. When trustees leave the board, they are more likely than ever to be reflective and willing to give you their frank opinions. The board chair or the Governance Committee chair should schedule a meeting with each retiring board member, asking questions such as these:

- What was the most important contribution you were able to make to the museum through your board service?
- Were there other things you wish you could have accomplished? If so, what got in your way?
- What was the biggest change in the board during your tenure?
- If you could change one thing about board meetings, what would it be?
- If a friend or colleague asked you for advice about joining the board, what would you tell them?
- How would you like to continue to support and be involved in the work of the museum?

This kind of feedback will help the Governance Committee improve board procedures for current members. It will also extend the relationship with former board members who continue to serve the museum as community representatives or on advisory boards. The Museum Trustee Association says that "properly handled, the exit interview can reinvigorate the departing trustee's relationship to the museum and its mission. Remember, it's easier to keep an old friend than to make a new one."[6]

The Governance Committee should also take responsibility for recognizing and thanking retiring board members. Taking the time during a board meeting or the annual meeting to summarize what each board member has done for the museum, thanking them for their service, and sharing a small gift are gracious ways to end a member's tenure.

INVEST THE TIME

If your board has no formal means of assessment, be assured that you are not alone. Many boards don't spend time evaluating their own performance. Perhaps that's because assessment takes time away from the other demands of governance, which often seem more pressing.

It's true that assessment takes time, but the leadership partnership is worth spending time on. When you consider the leveraging impact of boards, a few hours invested in assessing their effectiveness seems a small price to pay for improved performance that will benefit their institutions and the communities they serve.

Another reason that formal board assessment is rare is that few boards have the time or the expertise needed to create assessment instruments. These templates eliminate the front-end work of developing questionnaires and response tallies so boards can get right to the important work of reflecting on their individual and collective responses. Building on this framework, the administrator can tailor these instruments to the specific needs of their board.

We estimate that individual board members will spend twenty to thirty minutes completing each of the three questionnaires and a few hours discussing the findings at a board retreat. The board chair, the director, and members of the Executive or Governance Committee will spend several more hours reviewing the data and considering the strategic implications.

There's no doubt that these activities represent a significant investment of time and energy, but it is a small percentage of the total time the board spends in a year. A board of fifteen people that meets six times a year for two hours is devoting 180 hours annually to the collective work of governance. And that's just the beginning. Added to that is time spent in committee and task force meetings, participation in events, and individual board responsibilities. The time invested in the leadership partnership will pay big dividends in terms of board and director performance in the future. Like financial investments, the dividends can't begin to multiply until you jump into the market. So go ahead—get started now.

NOTES

1. Mary L. Hiland, "Transcending the Organization," *Nonprofit Quarterly*, Winter 2006.

2. BoardSource, *Museum Board Leadership 2017: A National Report* (Washington, DC: BoardSource, 2017), 15, 31.

3. Ibid., 23.

4. American Alliance of Museums, "Standards Regarding Institutional Mission Statements," accessed July 26, 2017, http://www.aam-us.org/resources/ethics-standards-and-best-practices/mission-and-planning.

5. Richard Chait, *How to Help Your Board Govern More and Manage Less* (Washington, DC: National Center for Nonprofit Boards, 1993), 10.

6. Museum Trustee Association, *Museum Trusteeship*, Summer 2001, 5.

1

Assess Individual Performance

BEGIN WITH THE INDIVIDUAL

Template 1: Individual Board Member Activity

The first template (not illustrated) is completed by the administrator or by a member of the committee or task force responsible for assessment. It should be updated regularly as new information becomes available from the development, membership, and volunteer departments. Each trustee should receive a copy of his or her report and be given the opportunity to make corrections, additions, or deletions if necessary. Trustees may also wish to review their data at the end of each fiscal year or the end of each board term.

To complete this template, the administrator will need to consult meeting minutes, committee and task force reports, and development office records. Start with the most recent calendar, fiscal, or program year, and then update annually. It may be difficult to collect information about prior years, but it's helpful to include whatever is available. Once this database is established, it will be easier to gather information going forward. The template includes the following fields:

- Board member name, the year first elected, the current term (first, second, etc.), the year the current term expires, and whether the member is eligible for reelection. This information is automatically transferred from the member profiles.
- Board Meetings Attended: the number of meetings attended, expressed as a proportion of the total (e.g., six of nine meetings, or 6/9).
- Membership Category: the appropriate option from your museum membership categories (e.g., family, contributing, sustaining, or donor).
- Committees/Task Forces: the list of committees on which this member serves, noting chairmanships.
- Fundraisers: the administrator will customize this list with the names of each fundraiser, noting the level of participation (e.g., committee chair, committee member, sponsor, event volunteer, guest, or purchased table).
- Contributions: customized list with the names of the appropriate funds (e.g., annual fund, endowment, acquisitions, or capital campaign) and completed with the member's level of giving. Ranges may be more appropriate than specific numbers.
- Solicitation: records contacts that resulted in new members or financial contributions (e.g., "2017: family business purchased a corporate membership" or "2016: secured a $5,000 contribution from the X Foundation").
- Other Participation and Support: includes other types of board service or in-kind contributions (e.g., "facilitated strategic planning retreat," "donated baseball tickets to the silent auction," or "provided software training services to staff").

Although the primary purpose of Template 1 is to record and monitor the participation of individual board members, compiling the activity reports of the entire board can also provide useful information. In the same way that good teachers view their students' report cards and progress reports as a reflection of their teaching effectiveness, the Governance Committee will find the combined responses of all **Individual Board Member Activity** reports a useful measure of its efficacy in promoting board participation.

The reports can be compared from year to year to note trends in board participation and contributions. For example, if financial contributions are increasing individually and collectively, that's a sign of growing board involvement and satisfaction. If participation in fundraisers is declining, the board may need to clarify its expectations or create incentives for more active participation. If board participation in any particular fundraiser is falling, the Development Committee may need to consider whether that event needs to be revitalized or replaced.

Take Note!

- Template 1 is marked "Confidential" to ensure the privacy of board records and maintain confidentiality about individual contributions. The Board Activity Report is to be seen only by the board member, the administrator, and the chair of the committee or task force undertaking the assessment.

TRUSTEE SELF-REFLECTION

Template 2: Self-Assessment

When it comes to evaluating the effectiveness of individual board members, the facts in **Individual Board Member Activity** are only half of the equation. One senior staff member says, "This tool measures the measurable. It doesn't really get to the subjective issues, to what's in board members' hearts. Your board can be performing to all of these requirements and still not be an effective board." Often the most important qualities are the hardest to measure. **Template 2: Self-Assessment** aims to address these more subjective aspects of trustee performance. It asks trustees to reflect on their own attitudes, effectiveness, and satisfaction with board service. They rate their agreement with twenty-nine statements in ten categories.

Gathering the Data

The surveys are available online in the museum's *Templates for Trustees* website, which is designed to make it convenient for trustees to access and complete them. The following steps will help lay the groundwork for their full and active participation:

- Discuss the process at a board meeting and include background and instructions in the board packet.
- Send requests and reminders by email, with clear instructions and directions for locating the Self-Assessment in the Template Library.
- Keep track of responses and send email reminders to those who have not responded within a week.

Instruct board members and the director to rate each statement on a scale from 5 (agree strongly) to 1 (disagree strongly). They can also choose 0 for "no opinion," which includes "not applicable" or "insufficient experience or information to respond." Remind respondents that there are no right or wrong answers. Improving board performance requires honesty, not high scores. The important thing is to be candid. It is best not to deliberate too long about each statement because the first response that comes to mind is usually the most valid and the most current. Board members should rate each statement in terms of their experiences during the past year only, not their entire tenure. The application will then weight each answer, creating an average score.

Template 2: Self-Assessment

I. Mission, Vision, and Strategy

1. I know the museum's mission statement well enough to paraphrase it.
2. The mission statement resonates for me personally and I believe in the goals of the museum.
3. I am familiar with the strategic plan and have thoughtfully considered what I can do to advance it.
4. I have an understanding and appreciation of the museum's institutional culture and a sense of its history.

II. Personal Development

5. I am personally committed to making the museum a more inclusive and welcoming place for people of all backgrounds.
6. The board manual and supplemental material given to me when I joined the board provided a good foundation for my board service.
7. I have sought out additional information about museums and nonprofit governance in print and online resources.
8. I take advantage of opportunities to network with colleagues on other nonprofit boards and/or attend conferences on museums and nonprofit governance.

III. Board Participation

9. There is a free and open exchange of information and ideas at board meetings; I feel comfortable asking questions and raising difficult issues.
10. I respect the confidentiality of all issues discussed in board meetings and board correspondence.
11. I have participated actively on one or more committees or task forces during the past year.
12. I feel that I have made a positive contribution to the work of the board through a combination of my knowledge, skills, expertise, and contacts with others.

IV. Individual-Board Relationship

13. As a new board member, I have sought out the advice of veteran board members.
14. As a veteran board member, I have reached out to help new board members.
15. There is a construction and open relationship between board members (new and veteran).

V. Individual-Staff Relationship

16. I have had opportunities to get to know the director through board work and social functions.
17. I have had opportunities to get to know key staff members and their areas of expertise.
18. I ensure that any dealings I have with individual staff members do not undermine the relationship between the director and his/her staff.

VI. Individual Oversight

19. I understand that my fiduciary responsibility is to hold the museum and its collections in trust for the public.
20. I understand the museum's code of ethics and consider it when making decisions about my actions on the board.
21. I have received the information and training I need to understand the legal, fiduciary, and ethical expectations and requirements of board service.

VII. Financial Oversight and Contributions

22. I have a clear understanding of the museum's financial situation and business model.
23. I have made financial contributions that met or exceeded the commitments I made when I joined the board.
24. I have supported fundraising efforts through a combination of identifying, cultivating, and soliciting donors and participating in museum fundraisers.

VIII. Collections Knowledge

25. I am familiar with the museum's collections and the policies and procedures in place to care for them.
26. I keep abreast of local, regional, national, and international developments in the area of the museum's collections and programs.

IX. Facilities

27. I am familiar with the museum's facilities, both public and behind-the-scenes.

X. Museum Advocate

28. I have served as an ambassador to individuals and groups in the community and identified opportunities for the museum to increase its visibility and impact.
29. I regularly attend exhibitions and programs with an interest in understanding how visitors perceive the museum and how the museum provides services to the community.

At the end of the questionnaire are two open-ended questions, the answers to which will be collected into a separate report:

30. The most rewarding aspect of being a member of this board is . . .
31. The most challenging aspect of being a member of this board is . . .

SELF-ASSESSMENT SUMMARIES

As data are entered into Template 2, the app compiles responses and calculates an average score for each statement and each category, creating detailed reports.

- **Survey Responses by Question**: the distribution and average of responses by question and by category.
- **Survey Responses by Member**: the responses (by numerical value) entered by each member for each question.
- **Responses to Open-Ended Questions**: the answers each member gave to the two open-ended questions.

Interpreting the Data: The Hypothetical Board

To illustrate how to interpret the data, we have included the responses of our hypothetical board throughout this volume. The reports illustrate issues that some boards may face and suggest ways they may be explored and addressed. Begin with some of the average scores for each category in **Survey Responses by Question**. In general, the higher the scores, the greater the board's sense of efficacy and satisfaction. Scores of 4 or above are highly affirmative; scores between 3.5 and 4 are positive; scores between 3 and 3.5 are worth watching; and scores below 3 are cause for concern. In any category with an average score of 3.5 or below, look at the scores for individual statements. Are the responses to most statements in that category consistently low, or are one or two statements with very low scores pulling the average down? If so, you may be able to identify the particular areas of concern. Here are four typical response patterns that require further investigation.

Example One: In figure 1.1, the average score of the Mission, Vision, and Strategy category is only 2.98, which is cause for concern. Looking at individual statements, it is clear that statement 4 (*I have an understanding and appreciation of the museum's institutional culture and a sense of its history*) elicited significantly lower scores, with an overall average of 2.08. The real issue, then, is not with the museum's strategic thinking but in a critical area of board development—understanding the museum's history—which suggests the need for board development activities that provide information and training in these areas.

Example Two: In figure 1.2, the average score for Individual-Board Relationship is also very low at 2.17. A review of the three statements for that category reveals that all twelve respondents gave ratings of "disagree strongly," "disagree," or "neutral," suggesting that personal relationships among the board need to be strengthened. Focusing solely on the business side of the board's functioning does not lead to healthy board dynamics. This board needs to get to know one another, particularly veteran and new members, and spend time socializing as well as meeting.

Example Three: In addition to looking at the averages, it is useful to look at the distribution of responses. Are there areas where there is a large disparity of opinion, experience, or perception? For example, the average response for the Individual-Staff Relationship category is relatively low at 3.17. In this case, the answers are fairly well distributed and all three statements have comparable ratings (figure 1.3).

That suggests that perhaps there is more to learn from the answers of individual board members in **Survey Responses by Member** (figure 1.4). That report shows that seven members consistently gave ratings of 4 or 5 but five members responded with 1 or 2. What might account for the marked discrepancy? Are members of some committees or other working groups in regular contact with the director and senior staff, an opportunity not available

			Count	Weight	Avg
1. Mission, Vision, and Strategy	1. I know the museum's mission statement well enough to paraphrase it.	Agree Strongly	1	5	5.00
		Agree	2	8	4.00
		Neutral	7	21	3.00
		Disagree	2	4	2.00
		Disagree strongly			
	1 Total		12	38	3.17
	2. The mission statement resonates for me personally and I believe in the goals of the museum.	Agree Strongly			
		Agree	5	20	4.00
		Neutral	6	18	3.00
		Disagree	1	2	2.00
		Disagree strongly			
	2 Total		12	40	3.33
	3. I am familiar with the strategic plan and have thoughtfully considered what I can do to advance it.	Agree Strongly			
		Agree	4	16	4.00
		Neutral	8	24	3.00
		Disagree			
		Disagree strongly			
	3 Total		12	40	3.33
	4. I have an understanding and appreciation of the museum's institutional culture and a sense of its history.	Agree Strongly			
		Agree			
		Neutral	3	9	3.00
		Disagree	7	14	2.00
		Disagree strongly	2	2	1.00
	4 Total		12	25	2.08
I Total			48	143	2.98

FIGURE 1.1

Self-Assessment Summary: Mission, Vision, and Strategy, Responses by Question (Courtesy of the Museum Trustee Association)

			Count	Weight	Avg
IV. Individual-Board Relationships	13. As a new board member, I have sought out the advice of veteran board members.	Agree Strongly			
		Agree			
		Neutral			
		Disagree	3	6	2.00
		Disagree strongly	1	1	1.00
	1 Total		4	7	1.75
	14. As a veteran board member, I have reached out to help new board members.	Agree Strongly			
		Agree			
		Neutral	2	6	3.00
		Disagree	5	10	2.00
		Disagree strongly	1	1	1.00
	2 Total		8	17	2.13
	15. There is a construction and open relationship between board members (new and veteran).	Agree Strongly			
		Agree			
		Neutral	5	15	3.00
		Disagree	6	12	2.00
		Disagree strongly	1	1	1.00
	3 Total		12	28	2.33
IV Total			24	52	2.17

FIGURE 1.2

Self-Assessment Summary: Individual-Board Relationship, Responses by Question (Courtesy of the Museum Trustee Association)

V. Individual-Staff Relationship	16. I have had opportunities to get to know the director through board work and social functions.	Agree Strongly	1	5	5.00
		Agree	5	20	4.00
		Neutral	1	3	3.00
		Disagree	4	8	2.00
		Disagree strongly	1	1	1.00
	1 Total		12	37	3.08
	17. I have had opportunities to get to know key staff members and their areas of expertise.	Agree Strongly	1	5	5.00
		Agree	5	20	4.00
		Neutral	1	3	3.00
		Disagree	4	8	2.00
		Disagree strongly	1	1	1.00
	2 Total		12	37	3.08
	18. I ensure that any dealings I have with individual staff members do not undermine the relationship between the director and his/her staff.	Agree Strongly	3	15	5.00
		Agree	3	12	4.00
		Neutral	1	3	3.00
		Disagree	5	10	2.00
		Disagree strongly			
	3 Total		12	40	3.33
V Total			36	114	3.17

FIGURE 1.3
Self-Assessment Summary: Individual-Staff Relationship, Responses by Question (Courtesy of the Museum Trustee Association)

to others? Is there a faction of the board that feels some antipathy or ambivalence toward the staff leadership? The board chair or chair of the committee or task force administering the assessments might engage the board in dialogue about those questions in an effort to determine why there is such a lack of consensus. In this case, where the questions are about relationships with the director and senior staff, the discussion should take place in executive session (if the museum is not bound by sunshine laws).

V. Individual-Staff Relationship	16. I have had opportunities to get to know the director through board work and social functions.	5	4	4	2	4	4	2	2	4	2	1	3
	17. I have had opportunities to get to know key staff members and their areas of expertise.	4	4	5	2	4	4	2	2	4	1	2	3
	18. I ensure that any dealings I have with individual staff members do not undermine the relationship between the director and his/her staff.	4	5	4	2	5	4	2	2	5	2	2	3

FIGURE 1.4
Self-Assessment Summary: Individual-Staff Relationship, Responses by Member (Courtesy of the Museum Trustee Association)

Example Four: You may also find that only one or two responses are widely separated from the group. Factors that can contribute to divergence of opinion include board tenure, participation on committees, and individual circumstances. Again, in **Survey Responses by Member**, notice that one respondent rated all the questions in the Personal Development category with a 1 or 2 (figure 1.5). Because the identity of each respondent is confidential, the committee has no way of knowing who is feeling so underprepared. But a general invitation for all members, regardless of tenure, to attend board orientation and receive an up-to-date board manual might help remedy this specific lapse.

	II. Personal Development	5. I am personally committed to making the museum a more inclusive and welcoming place for people of all backgrounds.	5	4	4	4	5	5	4	5	4	4	2	3
		6. The board manual and supplemental material given to me when I joined the board provided a good foundation for my board service.	5	3	3	3	4	4	5	3	4	5	1	2
		7. I have sought out additional information about museums and nonprofit governance in print and online resources.	4	3	4	4	5	5	4	5	3	5	1	3
		8. I take advantage of opportunities to network with colleagues on other nonprofit boards and/or attend conferences on museums and nonprofit governance.	5	4	3	5	3	4	5	3	3	5	2	3

FIGURE 1.5

Self-Assessment Summary: Personal Development, Responses by Member (Courtesy of the Museum Trustee Association)

Interpreting Open-Ended Questions

Although qualitative data are challenging to interpret, they can provide valuable insights into leadership issues. As noted above, there may be members of the board with skills and expertise in analyzing text, identifying common themes, and sorting responses into broad categories. You may enlist committee members in the process of reviewing and sorting responses. Online apps that create word clouds from blocks of text can also be useful for identifying the most commonly used words.

Comparing Results Year to Year

Administering the survey every year or every other year allows the board to track its progress, particularly around areas of concern or emphasis. For example, if the Governance Committee implements a new board development program, one would hope to see rising scores in those areas.

Take Note!

- Template 2 is marked "Confidential" to encourage candor. Assure trustees that their responses will be saved anonymously in the program. Results will be reported to the board in aggregate as overall averages.

2

Assess Board Performance

Board members looked within themselves to answer the questions in **Template 2: Self-Assessment**. Now they must look at their colleagues around the board table to answer the questions in **Template 3**. The director's views on board performance are also critical to the board assessment.

An assessment of board dynamics, routines, and policies can enhance the effectiveness of governance in any museum, regardless of what its current concerns are or where it stands in its institutional life cycle. (There are several good models of life cycles of nonprofit organizations. Susan Kenny Stevens's book *Nonprofit Lifecycles* is included in the **Resource Guide**.) Assessment can be especially useful during leadership transitions. Sharing assessment data with an incoming board chair can help the new chair and the Executive Committee to think strategically about board priorities, committee appointments, and meeting agendas. Sharing this information with a new director can help him or her get to know the board, supplementing personal introductions and providing an unbiased view of board leadership. For more information about orienting new directors, see *Executive Transitions,* volume 3 in the *Templates for Trustees* series.

MEASURE BOARD EFFECTIVENESS

Template 3: Board Assessment

This survey asks respondents to measure the effectiveness of the board as a whole by considering forty statements in ten categories related to museum governance. These categories and many of the subcategories are analogous to the ten categories in Templates 2 and 4, which examine the same functions from the standpoint of individual board members and the director (see table 0.1). The structure of the surveys emphasizes the importance of distinguishing between the board's sphere of responsibility and the director's role. However, things are sometimes ambiguous. With a nuanced understanding of their distinct but complementary roles, trustees and directors will be able to avoid arbitrary or artificial distinctions that can hamper effective leadership.

The Perspectives of the Executive Committee and the Director

Members of an active Executive Committee tend to have a slightly different perspective than the rest of the board because they interact frequently with the director and committee chairs and they may have longer tenure. That's why the Executive Committee's responses are reported separately on the reports in addition to being averaged in with the responses of the full board. If the Executive Committee's responses are markedly different from the responses of the board at large, it's important to ask why. Does leadership have its fingers on the pulse of the board? Is the Executive Committee privy to information the rest of the board is unaware of? Because the director

Template 3: Board Assessment

I. Mission, Vision, and Strategy

1. The board has been actively involved in articulating a mission statement that serves as a guide for board, staff, and volunteer activities.
2. The board understands the interests and needs of the museum's members, its visitors, and the communities it serves and has a vision of how the museum must evolve in order to remain relevant and vital to current and future supporters.
3. The museum has a strategic plan; uses it to guide decision-making, priority-setting and budgeting; and monitors progress on the plan.
4. The board knows the history and culture of the museum and understands what must be preserved to maintain its essence and integrity.

II. Board Membership and Development

5. The board reflects the diversity of the communities the museum aims to serve in terms of characteristics such as age, interests, points of view, racial, and ethnic background.
6. Board committees and task forces involve staff and community representatives as needed to incorporate a broad range of perspectives.
7. The recruitment and nomination process identifies and attracts new members with the perspectives and experience needed on the board.
8. The process for election of board officers identifies individuals with the experience, perspectives, and leadership skills needed to guide the board.
9. The board identifies and cultivates new leadership with an eye toward the future, providing opportunities to develop leadership skills.
10. Continuing education of board members is an ongoing priority for the board, which allocates time and resources for that purpose.

III. Board Operations

11. Board meetings are well organized and constructive; agendas and relevant information are sent well in advance; meetings begin and end promptly.
12. Board reports and consent agendas are clear and concise, telling trustees what they need to know to make well-informed decisions.
13. The majority of board discussions focus on policy and strategic issues (not operations).
14. The Executive Committee acts on behalf of the full board to improve efficiency while encouraging the active participation of all members.
15. Active board committees and task forces involve staff and community members, advancing the museum's strategic priorities.

IV. Board-Director Partnership

16. The board has defined the roles and responsibilities of the director in a written job description and developed an appropriate compensation package.
17. A board committee conducts an annual assessment of the director, monitoring progress on agreed-upon goals.
18. The board has a strong and effective working relationship with the director built on mutual respect and support.

V. Board-Staff Relationship

19. The board focuses its attention on policy issues, allowing staff to determine the most effective ways of implementing policy.
20. The board demonstrates respect for staff expertise and professionalism, carefully considering their advice on such issues as finance, development, collections, and education.
21. The board, or a board committee, has established personnel policies, including grievances, compensation, and benefits packages.
22. The board appreciates the roles that volunteers play and recognizes their contributions to the museum.

VI. Board Oversight

23. The board has created statements of purpose and bylaws as required by law and refers to them regularly, updating as needed.
24. The board has adopted and adheres to a code of ethics specific to the museum that governs individual and collective activities of trustees, staff, and volunteers.
25. The board or its officers keep abreast of legal, legislative, and regulatory requirements and ensure the museum's compliance.

VII. Financial Stewardship and Fundraising

26. The board ensures that current and projected financial resources will enable the museum to fulfill its mission and carry out its strategic plan.
27. The board receives regular financial reports that are complete, accurate, timely, and understandable.
28. The board, or a board committee, sets policy on the management of the museum's financial resources, including endowment funds and investments.
29. The board regularly obtains an independent audit that is complete and understandable from a reputable outside source.
30. The board's expectations for individual trustees' financial contributions and support of fundraising are clearly stated and understood.
31. The board and its committees work in concert with the director and development staff to identify and target resources and coordinate an effective fundraising program.

VIII. Collections Stewardship

32. The board views the collection as central to the museum's mission and serving the public.

33. The board has established appropriate policies and procedures to ensure that the physical plant meets all standards necessary to safeguard the permanent collection and temporary exhibitions.

34. Working with staff, the board, or a board committee, has articulated a collections policy that clearly defines the range, scope, and quality of the collection and provides guidelines for accessioning, deaccessioning, and lending of objects.

35. To maximize the potential of the collection, the board supports expanding public access through the creative use of new technology and other initiatives.

IX. Facilities Management

36. The board provides oversight for the operations and management of the building and grounds, ensuring a safe and secure environment for staff, visitors, and the collection.

37. The board approves all major changes and improvements in the physical plant to ensure that they are consistent with the budget, mission, and strategic plan.

X. Community Engagement

38. Board members act as liaisons to key groups and individuals in the community, gathering information on constituent needs and bringing this back to the board.

39. The board acts as an advocate for the museum, actively promoting its mission and programs to individuals and groups in the community.

40. Board members attend exhibitions and public programs with an interest in better understanding the perspective of museum visitors and how the museum might better serve the community.

has a unique perspective on board performance, his or her responses are reported separately and are not averaged in with those of board members.

Case in point: One experienced board member noted that although she considered herself an involved and diligent trustee, her perspective changed dramatically once she became president-elect: "I had chaired the Governance Committee and helped to resolve a major organizational challenge, so I thought I knew the place. But even with all that experience, once I became president-elect and started attending Executive Committee and Finance Committee meetings, my perspective on board issues broadened. I started to understand the fiscal issues far more clearly. I was privy to personnel questions that had been kept confidential. And my relationship with the executive director became closer but also more formal."

Gathering the Data

The surveys are completed online in the museum's *Templates for Trustees* website. Respondents can easily access and complete them with the following foundation.

- Discuss the process at a board meeting and include background and instructions in the board packet.
- Send requests and reminders by email, with clear instructions and directions for locating the Board Assessment in the online Template Library.
- Keep track of responses and send email reminders to those who have not responded within a week.

Instruct board members and the director to rate each statement on a scale from 5 (agree strongly) to 1 (disagree strongly). They can also choose 0 for "no opinion," which includes "not applicable" or "insufficient experience or information to respond." Remind respondents that there are no right or wrong answers. Improving board performance requires honesty, not high scores. The important thing is to be candid. It is best not to deliberate too long about each statement because the first response that comes to mind is usually the most valid and the most current.

Board members and the director should rate each statement in terms of their experiences during the past year only, not their entire tenure. The application will then weight each answer, creating an average score.

BOARD ASSESSMENT SUMMARIES

The online app will tally the data from each questionnaire on **Template 3: Board Assessment**, calculate an average score for each statement and each category, and create the following reports:

- **Survey Responses by Question**: the distribution and average of responses by question and by category.
- **Survey Responses by Group**: the distribution of responses by board members at-large, the Executive Committee, the full board, and the director (the report also calculates the difference between the scores of the full board and the director).
- **Survey Responses by Member**: the responses (as numerical values) entered by each member for each statement.
- **Responses to Open-Ended Questions**: the answers each member gave to the open-ended questions.

The assessment ends with three open-ended questions, the responses to which are collected in the above report:

41. What have been the board's three greatest achievements during the past year?
42. What have been the board's three greatest challenges during the past year?
43. Given the museum's mission and strategic goals, what do you see as the board's three highest priorities for the coming year?

Although qualitative data are challenging to interpret, they can provide valuable insights into important leadership issues. In the words of one director, "I like people to be able to express their thoughts rather than just agreement or disagreement." The board's and the director's responses to these questions must be considered carefully because they sum up their attitudes about board performance and priorities.

Comparing Board and Director Perspectives

To ensure that both sides of the leadership partnership are working in concert, it is critical to compare the board's and the director's responses. The online app will create **Survey Responses by Group** that compares the director's ratings with those of the board and calculates the difference between the two. A positive number means the board's average rating is lower than the director's, while a negative number means the board's average rating is higher than the director's. If most of the numbers in a particular category are negative, it would appear that the board has a more positive opinion than the director.

Interpreting the Data: The Hypothetical Board

The reports and comments in this section reflect the responses of our hypothetical board. In interpreting the responses, look first at the average scores for each category and each statement in **Survey Responses by Question**. In general, higher scores suggest that respondents have a greater sense of the board's effectiveness. Scores of 4 or above are highly affirmative; scores between 3.5 and 4 are positive; scores between 3 and 3.5 are worth watching; and scores below 3 are cause for concern.

This report will reveal some categories that bear further investigation. As with Template 2, looking at individual statements can shed light on category ratings.

II. Board Membership and Development					
5. The board reflects the diversity of the communities the museum aims to serve in terms of characteristics such as age, interests, points of view, racial, and ethnic background.	Agree Strongly			
	Agree			
	Neutral	1	3	3.00
	Disagree	9	18	2.00
	Disagree strongly	3	3	1.00
	No Opinion			
	1 Total	13	24	1.85
6. Board committees and task forces involve staff and community representatives as needed to incorporate a broad range of perspectives.	Agree Strongly			
	Agree			
	Neutral	1	3	3.00
	Disagree	7	14	2.00
	Disagree strongly	5	5	1.00
	No Opinion			
	2 Total	13	22	1.69
7. The recruitment and nomination process identifies and attracts new members with the perspectives and experience needed on the board.	Agree Strongly			
	Agree	6	24	4.00
	Neutral	7	21	3.00
	Disagree			
	Disagree strongly			
	No Opinion			
	3 Total	13	45	3.46
8. The process for election of board officers identifies individuals with the experience, perspectives, and leadership skills needed to guide the board.	Agree Strongly			
	Agree	4	16	4.00
	Neutral	9	27	3.00
	Disagree			
	Disagree strongly			
	No Opinion			
	4 Total	13	43	3.31
9. The board identifies and cultivates new leadership with an eye toward the future, providing opportunities to develop leadership skills.	Agree Strongly			
	Agree	6	24	4.00
	Neutral	5	15	3.00
	Disagree	2	4	2.00
	Disagree strongly			
	No Opinion			
	5 Total	13	43	3.31
10. Continuing education of board members is an ongoing priority for the board, which allocates time and resources for that purpose.	Agree Strongly			
	Agree	4	16	4.00
	Neutral	9	27	3.00
	Disagree			
	Disagree strongly			
	No Opinion			
	6 Total	13	43	3.31

FIGURE 2.1
Board Assessment Summary: Board Membership and Development, Responses by Question (Courtesy of the Museum Trustee Association)

Example One: Two statements in the Board Membership and Development category relate to areas that need attention (figure 2.1). Statement 5, with a score of just 1.85 (*The board reflects the diversity of the communities the museum aims to serve in terms of characteristics such as age, interests, points of view, racial, and ethnic background*), shines a spotlight on priorities the Governance Committee must keep in mind as it recruits new board members. Statement 6, with an even lower score of 1.69 (*Board committees and task forces involve staff and community representatives as needed to incorporate a broad range of perspectives*), suggests that the Governance Committee and committee chairs focus their energies on seeking new members for committees and task forces that reflect the many communities served by the museum. The other statements in this category are, in contrast, quite strong, with no one answering "disagree" or "strongly disagree."

Example Two: Three questions about board meetings in Board Operations (figure 2.2) evidence a sharp difference between the scores of the Executive Committee, which average 4.00 to 4.60, and the rest of the board, which range from 2.00 to 2.57. Clearly the experience of serving on the Executive Committee has a positive influence on perception of board operations. Why is that and how might the experience of other board members be improved?

Question ▼∧✕	Choice ▼∧✕		Board Member		Executive Committee	
			Count	Avg	Count	Avg
11. Board meetings are well-organized and constructive: agendas and relevant information are sent well in advance; meetings begin and end promptly.	Agree Strongly				3	5.00
	Agree				2	4.00
	Neutral		3	3.00		
	Disagree		4	2.00		
	Disagree strongly					
	No Opinion					
11 Total			7	2.43	5	4.60
12. Board reports and consent agendas are clear and concise, telling trustees what they need to know to make well-informed decisions.	Agree Strongly				1	5.00
	Agree				3	4.00
	Neutral		4	3.00	1	3.00
	Disagree		3	2.00		
	Disagree strongly					
	No Opinion					
12 Total			7	2.57	5	4.80
13. The majority of board discussions focus on policy and strategic issues (not operations).	Agree Strongly				2	5.00
	Agree				3	4.00
	Neutral					
	Disagree		7	2.00		
	Disagree strongly					
	No Opinion					
13 Total			7	2.00	5	4.40

FIGURE 2.2
Board Assessment Summary: Board Operations, Responses by Group (Courtesy of the Museum Trustee Association)

Example Three: Board-Staff Relationship has an average score of 3.13 and individual statement scores ranging from 2.77 to 3.85 (figure 2.3), which are moderately good scores. However, shifting to **Survey Responses by Member** tells a slightly different story. One member gave every statement in this category a score of 1 (figure 2.4). Because the survey is anonymous, there is no way of knowing who that is (and, again, it is unwise to speculate). Because the board's overall score of 3.13 is not particularly high, it might be wise to spend some time at a board meeting discussing all of the statements in this category. Start by creating a safe climate, and then encourage members to share their concerns, pointing out that issues cannot be addressed until they surface.

Survey Responses by Group for the hypothetical board reveals other ways that these reports can help diagnose issues with the board and director.

V. Board-Staff Relationship	Question	Choice			
	19. The board focuses its attention on policy issues, allowing staff to determine the most effective ways of implementing policy.	Agree Strongly	1	5	5.00
		Agree	4	16	4.00
		Neutral	3	9	3.00
		Disagree	4	8	2.00
		Disagree strongly	1	1	1.00
	1 Total		13	39	3.00
	20. The board demonstrates respect for staff expertise and professionalism, carefully considering their advice on such issues as finance, development, collections, and education.	Agree Strongly	2	10	5.00
		Agree	9	36	4.00
		Neutral	1	3	3.00
		Disagree			
		Disagree strongly	1	1	1.00
	2 Total		13	50	3.85
	21. The board, or a board committee, has established personnel policies, including grievances, compensation and benefits packages.	Agree Strongly	2	10	5.00
		Agree	2	8	4.00
		Neutral	3	9	3.00
		Disagree	5	10	2.00
		Disagree strongly	1	1	1.00
	3 Total		13	38	2.92
	22. The board appreciate the roles that volunteers play and recognizes their contributions to the museum.	Agree Strongly			
		Agree	3	12	4.00
		Neutral	5	15	3.00
		Disagree	4	8	2.00
		Disagree strongly	1	1	1.00
	4 Total		13	36	2.77
V Total			52	163	3.13

FIGURE 2.3
Board Assessment Summary: Board-Staff Relationship, Responses by Question (Courtesy of the Museum Trustee Association)

V. Board-Staff Relationship	19. The board focuses its attention on policy issues, allowing staff to determine the most effective ways of implementing policy.	3	2	5	2	3	4	2	3	2	4	4	1	4
	20. The board demonstrates respect for staff expertise and professionalism, carefully considering their advice on such issues as finance, development, collections, and education.	4	4	4	4	4	4	4	3	4	4	5	1	5
	21. The board, or a board committee, has established personnel policies, including grievances, compensation and benefits packages.	2	2	5	2	3	4	2	4	2	3	5	1	3
	22. The board appreciate the roles that volunteers play and recognizes their contributions to the museum.	2	2	3	2	3	4	3	4	2	3	3	1	4

FIGURE 2.4

Board Assessment Summary: Board-Staff Relationship, Responses by Member (Courtesy of the Museum Trustee Association)

Example Four: The board's and director's scores for Collections Stewardship show a significant difference in perception (figure 2.5). Board members are pleased with how they are meeting their obligations to care for the collection; however, the director scored each of the four statements with a 1. Statement 34 (*Working with staff, the board, or a board committee, has articulated a collections policy that clearly defines the range, scope, and quality of the collection and provides guidelines for accessioning, deaccessioning, and lending of objects*) suggests that it may be time for the Collections Committee to revisit the collections policy with input from curatorial staff. The low score on statement 35 (*To maximize the potential of the collection, the board supports expanding access through the creative use of new technology and other initiatives*) may signal the need for the board to consider staff recommendations to incorporate new technologies in opening up the museum's collection to real and virtual visitors.

Question ▼∧✕ Choice ▼∧✕		Board Member		Executive Committee		Executive Director		Member & Executive Com		Diff
		Count	Avg	Count	Avg	Count	Avg	Count	Avg	
32. The board views the collection as central to the museum's mission and serving the public.	Agree Strongly	2	5.00	2	5.00			4	5.00	
	Agree	5	4.00	3	4.00			8	4.00	
	Neutral									
	Disagree									
	Disagree strongly					1	1.00			
	No Opinion									
32 Total		7	4.29	5	4.40	1	1.00	12	4.33	-3.33
33. The board has established appropriate policies and procedures to ensure that the physical plant meets all standards necessary to safeguard the permanent collection and temporary exhibitions.	Agree Strongly	5	5.00	2	5.00			7	5.00	
	Agree	2	4.00	3	4.00			5	4.00	
	Neutral									
	Disagree									
	Disagree strongly					1	1.00			
	No Opinion									
33 Total		7	4.71	5	4.40	1	1.00	12	4.58	-3.58
34. Working with staff, the board, or a board committee, has articulated a collections policy that clearly defines the range, scope, and quality of the collection and provides guidelines for accessioning, deaccessioning, and lending of objects.	Agree Strongly	2	5.00	1	5.00			3	5.00	
	Agree	5	4.00	4	4.00			9	4.00	
	Neutral									
	Disagree									
	Disagree strongly					1	1.00			
	No Opinion									
34 Total		7	4.29	5	4.20	1	1.00	12	4.25	-3.25
35. To maximize the potential of the collection, the board supports expanding public access through creative use of new technology and other initiatives.	Agree Strongly	1	5.00	3	5.00			4	5.00	
	Agree	3	4.00	2	4.00			5	4.00	
	Neutral	3	3.00					3	3.00	
	Disagree									
	Disagree strongly					1	1.00			
	No Opinion									
35 Total		7	3.71	5	4.40	1	1.00	12	4.00	-3.00

FIGURE 2.5

Board Assessment Summary: Collections Stewardship, Responses by Group (Courtesy of the Museum Trustee Association)

Tracking Trends

Board trends are particularly important to consider because while board members come and go, the thread of governance extends without interruption regardless of individual personalities. We recommend saving the reports or printing them out and comparing responses from year to year.

Take Note!

- Remind respondents that "strongly agree" or "agree" doesn't mean they agree that the statement *should* be true but that they agree that it *is* true in the case of your board.

- Template 3 is marked "Confidential" to encourage candor. Assure those completing the survey that their responses will be recorded anonymously, and when findings are shared with the rest of the board, individual responses will not be distinguishable.
- The distribution of responses is important because an average score of 3.5 means one thing if the majority of responses fall between 3 and 4, whereas it means something very different if there are several 1s and 5s.

3

Assess Director Performance

MEASURE DIRECTOR PERFORMANCE

Template 4: Director Assessment

This template includes a survey and open-ended questions completed by individual board members and the director. It can be used alone as the basis for an annual review of the director's performance.[1] However, it is more revealing when used in conjunction with **Template 3: Board Assessment**, which provides a review of both arms of the leadership partnership. Since the director and the board work as a team, it is hard to explore the performance of one player without looking at the strengths and weaknesses of the other.

Assessing the director's performance benefits not only the leadership partners but also staff and volunteers. Staff members benefit from knowing that their leader is accountable for achieving performance goals just as they are. Volunteers, such as docents, are more comfortable with performance reviews when they see them as part of the museum's institutional culture. But perhaps no one stands to gain more from regular assessment of performance than the director. Robert Andringa explains, "Of course, every CEO is evaluated constantly in the minds of board members, staff, volunteers, donors, and beneficiaries of the organization's services. But when there are no common assumptions about the criteria for evaluation and no process that lets the unspoken become known, a CEO is really risking a lot by not insisting upon a periodic evaluation."[2] Though some board members may feel reluctant to evaluate their director's performance, they are actually doing the director a great disservice if they fail to fulfill this essential responsibility.

The Director Assessment, like the Board Assessment, incorporates perspectives from both the boardroom and the executive office. The director has an opportunity to assess his or her own performance by answering the same questions as the board. The director's responses are reported separately, and they are not averaged in with the board's responses.

The board and the director will be asked to evaluate the director's performance by agreeing or disagreeing with forty statements in ten categories related to museum governance. These categories are analogous to the ten categories in **Template 3: Board Assessment**, which examines the same functions from the standpoint of the board's roles (see table 0.1). The director is responsible for making day-to-day decisions and managing the staff while the board is responsible for setting policy. This sounds simple enough, but distinguishing between management and policy is a challenge for many director-board partnerships. Considering individual statements will help clarify the director's roles.

Comparing and contrasting the distinct but complementary responsibilities outlined in each category will suggest the appropriate focus for the director and the board. For example, category III in the Director Assessment focuses on the director's role in board meetings: providing the board with accurate information in a timely fashion,

Template 4: Director Assessment

I. Mission, Vision, and Strategy

1. The director has been actively involved in articulating a mission statement that serves as a guide for board, staff, and volunteer activities.
2. The director understands and appreciates the interests and needs of the museum's members, its volunteers, its visitors, and the communities it serves and has a vision of how the museum must evolve in order to remain relevant and vital to current and future supporters.
3. The director has worked with the board to create a strategic plan; uses it to guide decision-making, priority-setting and budgeting; and monitors progress on the plan.
4. The director knows the history and culture of the museum and understands what must be preserved to maintain its essence and integrity.

II. Staff and Board Development

5. The director has led hiring and recruitment efforts to ensure that the staff and volunteers reflect the diversity of the communities the museum aims to serve in terms of characteristics such as age, interests, points of view, racial, and ethnic background.
6. The size of the staff is appropriate for the work that must be done to meet the museum's needs.
7. Staff organization reflects the museum's strategic priorities.
8. The director demonstrates knowledge of effective personnel management techniques.
9. The director allocates time and resources for staff development, such as special training, retreats, visits with colleagues, and attendance at conferences.
10. The director effectively supports the continuing education of the board on trends and issues in museum practice as well as specific issues facing this museum.

III. Board Meetings

11. The director's report or consent agenda makes good use of trustees' time, prioritizing strategic issues over day-to-day management issues.
12. The director frames significant questions to guide board discussions and decisions.
13. The director solicits trustees' participation in strategic decisions and carefully considers their opinions and recommendations.
14. The director works with the Executive Committee to advance board agendas between regular board meetings.

IV. Director-Board Partnership

15. The director and board chair have developed effective methods for information sharing, issues clarification, and problem solving.
16. The director's annual review is timely and thoughtful, identifying specific strengths and areas for improvement and noting progress from year to year.
17. Mutual respect, trust, and support characterize the relationship between the director and the board.
18. The constructive and open working relationship between board members and the director maximizes efficiencies in both arms of governance.

V. Staff Management

19. The director establishes systems for communication and dialogue between staff and trustees so the board has a good knowledge of the workings of the museum.
20. The director facilitates effective working relationships between senior staff/department heads and board officers/committee chairs with common goals.
21. The director selects and cultivates qualified senior staff, encouraging the development of best museum practices and leadership skills.
22. The director effectively handles all staff issues, including grievances, in keeping with institutional policies.

VI. Director Oversight

23. The director ensures that there are appropriate administrative and operational systems in place to maintain the museum's collection, buildings, and grounds.
24. The director leads the staff effectively in the implementation of the strategic plan.
25. The director, with the help of the museum's legal counsel, keeps abreast of legal, legislative, and regulatory requirements and works with staff to ensure compliance.

VII. Financial Planning and Resource Development

26. The director works in concert with the board and staff to develop a realistic balanced annual operating budget that reflects the strategic priorities of the museum.
27. The director monitors the annual operating budget, making periodic reports to the board and revising the budget as needed.
28. The director supervises a financial staff that is knowledgeable and can explain financial issues in a user-friendly manner that facilitates good decision-making.
29. The director has established a system linking strategic and operational planning with budgeting.

30. The director guides revenue generation activities, including museum shops, cafes, and new product development, to maximize earned income.
31. The director works in concert with the board and development staff to effectively identify and target resources and implement a continuous fundraising program that supports the strategic plan and ensures a sustainable future for the museum.

VIII. Collections Management

32. Working with staff, the director ensures the physical care of the collection, in keeping with the museum's mission and standards of professional practice.
33. The director ensures that there are appropriate collections, registration, conservation, and research systems in place to use the collection to its fullest advantage.
34. The director demonstrates knowledge of and compliance with all necessary legal and ethical requirements for acquiring, lending, and disposing of the museum's collection.
35. The director works with staff to expand access to collections through creative use of new technology and other initiatives.

IX. Facilities Management

36. The director demonstrates knowledge of building operations and facilities management issues and establishes appropriate systems for the safety of the public.
37. The director involves the board in discussion and decision-making regarding facilities utilization, remodeling, and renovation.

X. Public Engagement

38. The director ensures that there are appropriate exhibitions, interpretation, and programs in place to attract and engage a growing and increasingly diverse audience.
39. The director has an excellent reputation in the local community and serves as a good ambassador for the museum with community and business leaders, public officials, funders, and collectors.
40. The director has an excellent reputation in the larger field, participating actively in museum conferences and other professional endeavors.

making good use of trustees' time by framing significant questions, and focusing on strategic issues rather than management decisions in board reports. Category III in the Board Assessment focuses on the board's role: being well prepared for meetings, creating a climate that makes it possible to discuss issues openly, cooperating and working as a team, and focusing on the decision-making process as well as the decisions. With these guidelines in mind, directors and trustees will be able to work in concert, avoiding arbitrary distinctions that can hamper effective leadership.

As with Templates 2 and 3, instruct board members and the director to rate each statement on a scale from 5 (agree strongly) to 1 (disagree strongly). They can also choose 0 for "no opinion," which includes "not applicable" or "insufficient experience or information to respond." Remind respondents that there are no right or wrong answers. Improving board performance requires honesty, not high scores. The important thing is to be candid. It is best not to deliberate too long about each statement because the first response that comes to mind is usually the most valid and the most current. Board members and the director should rate each statement in terms of their experiences during the past year only, not their entire tenure. The application will then weight each answer, creating an average score.

Who Can Best Assess the Director?

In the interest of encouraging full board participation in this mutual assessment process, **Template 4: Director Assessment** is completed by all trustees and the director. Reflecting on concrete, measurable aspects of the director's performance will help board members appreciate the many responsibilities of the museum's chief executive.

A March 2015 survey of nonprofit executive directors in Vermont and New Hampshire produced discouraging feedback on performance reviews. While every executive director agreed with the statement "The board of directors is supposed to review . . . performance annually," only 12 percent thought their boards had done an excellent job on their review. In a larger survey by CompassPoint, 45 percent of the executive directors reported that they had not had a performance evaluation during the last twelve months, and only 18 percent described their review as very useful.[3]

Having the entire board assess the director may not be appropriate in all museums. Some directors may be uncomfortable with the notion that each and every member of the board is his or her boss. And some boards may believe that not all of their members have enough direct experience with the director to measure performance. This is most likely to be true in larger institutions with large, multitiered boards or boards that have had an influx of new members. In these cases, it may make more sense for the director to be evaluated by the Executive Committee, whose members have more frequent contact with the director, or the Personnel Committee, which has specific responsibility for addressing staff issues, or perhaps by all committee chairs.

Gathering the Data

The templates are completed online in the museum's *Templates for Trustees* website. It is important to make it convenient and easy for trustees to access and complete the templates, following the same guidelines as the instructions for Template 3 (see page 17).

DIRECTOR ASSESSMENT SUMMARIES

The online app will tally the data from each survey on **Template 4: Director Assessment**, calculate an average score for each statement and each category, and create detailed reports.

- **Survey Responses by Question**: the distribution and average of responses by question and by category.
- **Survey Responses by Group**: the distribution of responses by board members at-large, the Executive Committee, the full board, and the director (the report calculates the difference between the scores of the full board and the director).
- **Survey Responses by Member**: the responses (by numerical value) entered by each member for each question.
- **Responses to Open-Ended Questions**: the answers each member gave to the open-ended questions.

At the end of the assessment are three open-ended questions, the responses to which are collected in a separate report.

41. What have been the director's three greatest achievements during the past year?
42. What have been the director's three greatest challenges during the past year?
43. Given the museum's mission and strategic goals, what do you see as the director's three highest priorities for the coming year?

Interpreting the Data: The Hypothetical Board

Example One: As noted above, the hypothetical board had consistently high ratings for the statements in the Collections Stewardship category of **Template 3: Board Assessment**, particularly when contrasted with the director's overall rating of 1 ("strongly disagree") across all four statements. The disparity is even more pronounced when compared with the board's ratings in the comparable Collections Management category (statements 32–35) of **Template 4: Director Assessment** (figure 3.1). The board ratings are between 1.75 and 2.83, while the director rated every question 4. Both sides of the partnership seem to have concerns about the other's work when it comes to care and use of the collections! This is obviously a topic for further discussion. It might reveal that the director and the board have different understandings of the museum's deaccessioning policies or contrasting notions of how technology should be employed to increase the use of the collection.

Question ▼∧✕	Choice ▼∧✕	Board Member		Executive Committee		Executive Director		Member & Executive Com		Diff
		Count	Avg	Count	Avg	Count	Avg	Count	Avg	
32. Working with staff, the director ensures the physical care of the collection, in keeping with the museum's mission and standards of professional practice.	Agree Strongly									
	Agree			1	4.00	1	4.00	1	4.00	
	Neutral	3	3.00	1	3.00			4	3.00	
	Disagree	4	2.00	3	2.00			7	2.00	
	Disagree strongly									
	No Opinion									
32 Total		7	2.43	5	2.60	1	4.00	12	2.58	1.58
33. The director ensures that there are appropriate collections, registration, conservation, and research systems in place to use the collection to its fullest advantage.	Agree Strongly									
	Agree					1	4.00			
	Neutral			1	3.00			1	3.00	
	Disagree	3	2.00	4	2.00			7	2.00	
	Disagree strongly	4	1.00					4	1.00	
	No Opinion									
33 Total		7	1.43	5	2.20	1	4.00	12	1.75	2.25
34. The director demonstrates knowledge of and compliance with all necessary legal and ethical requirements for acquiring, lending, and disposing of the museum's collection.	Agree Strongly									
	Agree					1	4.00			
	Neutral	4	3.00	3	3.00			7	3.00	
	Disagree	3	2.00	2	2.00			5	2.00	
	Disagree strongly									
	No Opinion									
34 Total		7	2.57	5	2.60	1	4.00	12	2.58	1.42
35. The director works with staff to expand access to collections through creative use of new technology and other initiatives.	Agree Strongly									
	Agree			1	4.00	1	4.00	1	4.00	
	Neutral	5	3.00	3	3.00			8	3.00	
	Disagree	2	2.00	1	2.00			3	2.00	
	Disagree strongly									
	No Opinion									
35 Total		7	2.71	5	3.00	1	4.00	12	2.83	1.17

FIGURE 3.1

Director Assessment Summary: Collections Management, Responses by Group (Courtesy of the Museum Trustee Association)

Example Two: Another glaring discrepancy in **Survey Responses by Group** is in the Director Oversight category (statements 23–25), where the director posted all 5s and the board's ratings range from 3.33 to 3.67 (figure 3.2). The differences in perspective on statements 23 (*The director ensures that there are appropriate administrative and operational systems in place to maintain the museum's collection, buildings, and grounds*) and 24 (*The director leads the staff effectively in the implementation of the strategic plan*) should be the starting point for a conversation between the director and the Executive or Personnel Committee. To plumb issues surrounding statement 25 (*The*

Question ▼∧✕	Choice ▼∧✕	Board Member		Executive Committee		Executive Director		Member & Executive Com		Diff
		Count	Avg	Count	Avg	Count	Avg	Count	Avg	
23. The director ensures that there are appropriate administrative and operational systems in place to maintain the museum's collection, buildings and grounds.	Agree Strongly			2	5.00	1	5.00	2	5.00	
	Agree	3	4.00	2	4.00			5	4.00	
	Neutral	3	3.00					3	3.00	
	Disagree	1	2.00	1	2.00			2	2.00	
	Disagree strongly									
	No Opinion									
23 Total		7	3.29	5	4.00	1	5.00	12	3.58	1.42
24. The director leads the staff effectively in the implementation of the strategic plan.	Agree Strongly	1	5.00	1	5.00	1	5.00	2	5.00	
	Agree	1	4.00	2	4.00			3	4.00	
	Neutral	4	3.00	1	3.00			5	3.00	
	Disagree	1	2.00					1	2.00	
	Disagree strongly			1	1.00			1	1.00	
	No Opinion									
24 Total		7	3.29	5	3.40	1	5.00	12	3.33	1.67
25. The director, with the help of the museum's legal counsel, keeps abreast of legal, legislative, and regulatory requirements and works with staff to ensure compliance.	Agree Strongly	4	5.00	2	5.00	1	5.00	6	5.00	
	Agree			1	4.00			1	4.00	
	Neutral			1	3.00			1	3.00	
	Disagree	3	2.00					3	2.00	
	Disagree strongly			1	1.00			1	1.00	
	No Opinion									
25 Total		7	3.71	5	3.60	1	5.00	12	3.67	1.33

FIGURE 3.2

Director Assessment Summary: Director Oversight, Responses by Group (Courtesy of the Museum Trustee Association)

director, with the help of the museum's legal counsel, keeps abreast of legal, legislative, and regulatory requirements and works with staff to ensure compliance), it may be helpful to involve the museum's attorney.

Example Three: The director's low score on statement 15 (*The director and board chair have developed effective methods for information sharing, issues clarification, and problem solving*) implies that from his or her perspective clearer communication could strengthen the leadership partnership.

Given the critical importance of the relationship between the board chair and director, a diligent board chair (particularly if new to the position) would initiate efforts to improve his or her individual relationship with the director and look for ways to develop a more constructive relationship with the board as whole.

Question ▼∧✕ Choice ▼∧✕		Board Member		Executive Committee		Executive Director		Member & Executive Com		Diff
		Count	Avg	Count	Avg	Count	Avg	Count	Avg	
▼ 15. The director and board chair have developed effective methods for information sharing, issues clarification, and problem solving.	Agree Strongly	4	5.00	1	5.00			5	5.00	
	Agree	2	4.00	2	4.00			4	4.00	
	Neutral	1	3.00	2	3.00			3	3.00	
	Disagree					1	2.00			
	Disagree strongly									
	No Opinion									
15 Total		7	4.43	5	3.80	1	2.00	12	4.17	-2.17

FIGURE 3.3
Director Assessment Summary: Director-Board Partnership, Responses by Group (Courtesy of the Museum Trustee Association)

After comparing numerical scores to the forty statements, it will also be interesting to compare the dispersion of priorities identified by the director and the board in response to the open-ended questions, particularly the identification of priorities for the coming year. This comparison will reveal how clear the communication is between the director and the board. Are the board's priorities for the director consistent, or is the board divided on where the director should focus his or her attention? Does the director understand the board's priorities? If the board's priorities for the director are in keeping with the director's own priorities, the leadership partnership is working as a team. If the board's priorities are markedly different from the director's, the two may not be playing the same game.

Take Note!
- Template 4 is marked "Confidential" to encourage candor. Assure those completing the survey that their responses will be recorded anonymously, and when findings are shared with the rest of the board, individual responses will not be distinguishable.
- Repeating the survey every year or every other year allows a board to track its performance over time.
- Remind respondents that "strongly agree" or "agree" doesn't mean they agree that the statement *should* be true but that they agree that it *is* true in the case of your director.

NOTES

1. If this tool will be the basis for the director's annual review, we recommend that it not be tied to a salary review, which falls more appropriately within the annual budget review process. Separating the director's performance review from compensation discussions provides for greater objectivity.

2. Robert Andringa, "Evaluations of CEOs by Their Boards," CEO Dialogues, Inc., 1993, 2.

3. Curtis R. Welling and John H. Vogel Jr., "A Practical (and Possibly Provocative) Approach to Leadership Transitions," *Nonprofit Quarterly*, May 21, 2015.

4

Develop a Leadership Plan

THE IMPORTANCE OF PLANNING AND DIALOGUE

Having completed these assessments, the board will benefit from an opportunity to look at the results and set goals for their collaborative work with the director. Having identified the critical issues in their partnership, they will be able to answer two questions:

- What steps can we take to individually and collectively strengthen the board's performance in the upcoming year?
- What steps can we take to individually and collectively strengthen the director's performance in the upcoming year?

This approach to planning is process oriented, not prescriptive. It is based on the knowledge and wisdom that exist on each individual board, not on advice from experts in nonprofit governance. Asking the right questions and exploring the answers together will lead to an approach that is right for each museum. In fact, the process is every bit as important as the resulting plan because it provides the opportunity for board members and the director to address issues of mutual concern. It encourages museum leaders to do their talking in the meeting room rather than in the parking lot.

It is best to set aside a special time and place for this dialogue and planning to occur. When people are in familiar settings they often assume familiar roles and behave in familiar ways. A half-day retreat in a relaxed setting other than the boardroom will allow voices that may not have been heard and views that may not have been aired to come to the surface.

The committee or task force charged with administering these assessments and working with the results should devote time and energy to thoughtful planning of the retreat. At times it may be helpful to bring in an outside facilitator. The person who facilitates the retreat should review the summary reports generated by **Template 3: Board Assessment** and **Template 4: Director Assessment** as well as the slides in the presentation before the meeting.

The presentation is in the most neutral theme available in PowerPoint: sans serif black type on a white background. Switching to a theme, color scheme, or typeface consistent with your museum's graphical identity and brand will make the presentation feel more familiar and inspiring.

Dialogue or Discussion?

The goal of the retreat is to encourage a dialogue rather than a discussion between board members and the director. Though these two words may seem synonymous, there are subtle but profound differences. In a discussion, you advocate in an effort to convince others of your perspective. In a dialogue, you ask questions in an effort to better understand perspectives that are different from your own. Having completed the assessment instruments, everyone will already know their own feelings about the performance of the board and the director. To leave the retreat with new information, they must focus their energies on asking and listening rather than telling.

The ultimate goal of the dialogue is to arrive at consensus about the priorities for strengthening the leadership partnership at your museum. But, as we know, consensus may not always be possible on all issues. If it is not, your board members and director can still gain an increased appreciation for the perspectives of others seated around the table. Everyone will perform better with a deeper understanding of views that differ from their own.

FROM ASSESSMENT TO PLANNING

Template 5: The Leadership Plan

The final template is a presentation (figure 4.1) that summarizes the data gathered from the Board Assessment and the Director Assessment. It is designed to bring the findings of these two assessments into focus and to help

FIGURE 4.1
The Leadership Plan: Slide Presentation (Courtesy of the Museum Trustee Association)

Director Assessment
Category Averages

Director Assessment
Strengths/Weaknesses

- Strengths (highest scores)
  - First
  - Second
- Weaknesses (lowest scores)
  - First
  - Second

Director Assessment
Discussion Questions

- How will these strengths help the director lead the museum?
- How can the director build on these strengths?
- How are these weaknesses impacting museum leadership?
- How can the board help the director overcome these weaknesses?

Director Assessment
Divergence of Opinion

- Trustees & the director have different views of
  - category or statement and ratings
  - category or statement and ratings
  - category or statement and ratings

Director Assessment
Divergence of Opinion

- How can the board support the leadership partnership with a better understanding of director's views?
- How can the director support the leadership partnership with a better understanding of the board's views?

What are the highest priorities for the work of the board?

Board	Director
1.	1.
2.	2.
3.	3.

The Leadership Plan

- During the next year, we will strengthen the board's performance in our areas of priority by....
  - Enter action step here
  - Enter action step here
  - Enter action step here

What are the highest priorities for the work of the director?

Board	Director
1.	1.
2.	2.
3.	3.

The Leadership Plan

- During the next year, we will strengthen the director's performance in our areas of priority by....
  - Enter action step here
  - Enter action step here
  - Enter action step here

Assess the Assessment

- How useful has this process been?
- How can we improve the assessment process for next year?

the board and the director draw out the most significant aspects of their responses. The slides will guide a dialogue about the strengths and weaknesses and the different perspectives of each leadership partner.

- Slide 1: The title slide can be customized with the museum's name, logo, and/or an image.
- Slide 2: The presentation begins with the museum's mission statement and vision statement (if there is one). Mission is so central to leadership that it is the first area measured on both the Board Assessment and the Director Assessment. If the dialogue stalls at any point, it may help to go back to this slide for a minute and ask, "What's most relevant here, given our mission?"
- Slide 3: The next slide provides talking points about the leadership partnership, stressing the importance of teamwork in challenging times. You may want to highlight the greatest challenges your museum is currently facing.
- Slide 4: This slide distinguishes between discussion and dialogue. To emphasize the truth of individual perspectives, you may want to try the following exercise. Hold up a multicolored beach ball between two people seated on opposite sides of the table. Ask each person to describe what they see, and then ask for clarification with questions such as "How much blue do you see? Is it light blue or dark blue? What color do you see to the left of the blue?" This simple exercise will illustrate that the same object looks different depending on individual perspectives.
- Slide 5: The Board Assessment is summarized in a graph showing the board's average rating for each category. The data for this graph can be drawn from the report **Survey Responses by Question**.
- Slide 6: Use the same report to identify and fill in the board's greatest strengths (the two categories with the highest average scores) and weaknesses (the two with the lowest scores).
- Slide 7: This slide asks four questions about strengths and weaknesses. You can use these general discussion questions, or you can articulate questions related to the specific strengths and challenges listed on the previous slide. For example, if Board Membership and Development receives a low score, you might ask, "How could changing our recruitment and nomination process help us to build a board capable of advancing our mission?"
- Slides 8 and 9: Slide 8 highlights those categories or individual statements where the assessment of the board and director were most divergent on the report **Survey Responses by Group**. Don't assume that areas of disagreement are problems. Those responses that reflect the widest range of opinion often lead to the most fruitful dialogues. Choose the three categories or statements with the highest numbers (either positive or negative) and pose questions that will stimulate a dialogue between the board and the director, leading to a better understanding of all perspectives. You can use the general discussion questions on slide 9 or articulate your own questions to address specific areas of incongruence.
- Slides 10–14: These slides look at comparable data from the Director Assessment and pose similar questions.
- Slide 15: The two lists on slide 15 are not drawn from a single source in *The Leadership Partnership* templates. Rather, the committee or task force charged with strengthening the partnership should select the three highest priorities for the board and the director after reviewing all of the reports, focusing on points of divergence and consensus. They should pay special attention to board members' and the director's answers to open-ended questions, particularly question 43 in **Template 3: Board Assessment**: *Given the museum's mission and strategic goals, what do you see as the board's two highest priorities for the coming year and why?* Alternatively, the committee could share all of the responses to the open-ended questions with the full board and generate these lists as a group at the retreat.
- Slide 16: If a board is going to invest the time and effort in assessing its performance and reflecting on the responses, it should take the next step: creating a plan to build on successes and make necessary improvements. On this slide the group identifies three action steps (with deadlines and assignment of responsibility wherever

possible) to strengthen the board's performance during the next year. The Executive Committee should leave these three bullet points open and complete the action plan as part of the meeting.

- Slides 17 and 18: These slides repeat the process of identifying priorities and action steps for the work of the director. Again, the perspectives of the board and the director are compared on slide 17, and action steps are summarized on slide 18. One source of ideas for the lists on slide 17 is the responses to question 43 on **Template 4: Director Assessment**: *Given the museum's mission and strategic goals, what do you see as the director's two highest priorities for the coming year and why?*
- Slide 19: The final slide invites the board to reflect on the entire assessment process and the development of the leadership plan. Was the mutual assessment process useful and how could it be improved in the future? Was the timing optimum given your museum's fiscal year, or should the process be scheduled somewhere else in the annual calendar? Did the statements reflect current issues at your museum, or do you need to change the wording of some? Use the answers to these questions to plan the assessment process for the following year.

A retreat organized around a comprehensive program of assessment and reflection puts the leadership team on a path of continuous improvement. This is central not only to improving the performance of the board but also to improving the organization as a whole. Reflection and strategic thinking are key to building the museum's capacity to learn, change, and grow.

Resource Guide for
The Leadership Partnership

PUBLICATIONS

Carver, John. *Boards That Make a Difference: A New Design for Leadership in Nonprofit and Public Organizations*, 3rd ed. San Francisco, CA: Jossey-Bass, 2006.

Chait, Richard P., Thomas P. Holland, and Barbara E. Taylor. *Improving the Performance of Governing Boards*. Phoenix, AZ: Oryx Press, 1996.

Charan, Ram, Michael Useem, and Dennis Carey. *Boards That Lead: When to Take Charge, When to Partner, and When to Stay Out of the Way*. Boston, MA: Harvard Business School Publishing Corporation, 2014.

Garry, Joan. *Joan Garry's Guide to Nonprofit Leadership: Because Nonprofits Are Messy*. Hoboken, NJ: John Wiley & Sons, 2017.

Grace, Kay Sprinkle. *The Ultimate Board Member's Book*. Medfield, MA: Emerson & Church, 2013.

Herman, Robert D., and Richard D. Heimovics. *Executive Leadership in Nonprofit Organizations: New Strategies for Shaping Executive-Board Dynamics*. San Francisco, CA: Jossey-Bass, 1991.

Hiland, Mary. "The Board Chair–Executive Director Relationship: Dynamics That Create Value for Nonprofit Organizations," *Journal for Nonprofit Management*, 2008. Accessed July 26, 2017. https://www.wwcc.edu/CMS/fileadmin/PDF/Learning_Center/board-chair-executive-director-relationship-hiland-scnm-journal08-2.pdf.

Houle, Cyril O. *Governing Boards: Their Nature and Nurture*. San Francisco, CA: Jossey-Bass, 1997.

Howe, Fisher. *The Nonprofit Leadership Team: Building the Board–Executive Director Partnership*. San Francisco, CA: Jossey-Bass, 2003.

Independent Sector. *Principles for Good Governance and Ethical Practice. A Guide for Charities and Foundations*. Washington, DC: Independent Sector, 2015. Accessed July 26, 2017. https://www.independentsector.org/resource/principles-preview/.

Ingram, Richard T. *Ten Basic Responsibilities of Nonprofit Boards*, 2nd ed. Washington, DC: BoardSource, 2015.

Ingram, Richard T., and William A. Weary. *Presidential and Board Assessment in Higher Education: Purposes, Policies, and Strategies*. Washington, DC: Association of Governing Boards of Universities and Colleges, 2000.

Katcher, Robin, Susan Gross, Karl Mathiasen, and Neel Master. *Boards Matter: Board Building Tools for the Busy Social Justice Executive*. Washington, DC: Management Assistance Group, 2007. Accessed July 28, 2017. http://www.managementassistance.org/board-building-tools-social-justice.

Management Consultants for the Arts. *The Board: A Challenge to Serve*. Stamford, CT: Management Consultants for the Arts, 2000. Accessed July 26, 2017. http://www.mcaonline.us/index.php?option=com_k2&view=item&id=187:the-board&Itemid=514.

———. *The Chair: More Than Just a Title*. Stamford, CT: Management Consultants for the Arts, 2001. Accessed July 26, 2017. http://www.mcaonline.us/index.php?option=com_k2&view=item&id=190:the-chair&Itemid=516.

Mott, William R. *Super Boards*. Self-Published, 2014.

O'Connell, Brian. *Operating Effective Committees*. Washington, DC: Independent Sector, 1988.

Poister, Theodore H., Maria P. Aristigueta, and Jeremy L. Hall. *Managing and Measuring Performance in Public and Nonprofit Organizations: An Integrated Approach*. San Francisco, CA: Jossey-Bass, 2014.

Roche, Nancy, and Jaan Witehead, eds. *The Art of Governance: Boards in the Performing Arts*. New York: Theater Communications Group, 2005.

Ryan, William P., Richard P. Chait, and Barbara E. Taylor. "Problem Boards or Board Program?" *Nonprofit Quarterly*, May 8, 2017. Accessed July 28, 2017. https://nonprofitquarterly.org/2017/05/08/problem-boards-or-board-problem/.

Shapiro, Michael. *Eleven Museums, Eleven Directors: Conversations on Art & Leadership*. Atlanta, GA: High Museum of Art, 2016.

Stevens, Susan Kenny. *Nonprofit Lifecycles: Stage-based Wisdom for Nonprofit Capacity*. St. Paul, MN: Stagewise Enterprises, 2002.

ORGANIZATIONS

Alliance for Nonprofit Management, 1732 1st Avenue, #28522, New York, NY 10128. Phone: 888-776-2434. Website: www.allianceonline.org.

American Alliance of Museums, 2451 Crystal Drive, Suite 1005, Arlington, VA 22202. Phone: 202-289-1818. Website: www.aam-us.org.

Association of Governing Boards of Universities and Colleges, 1133 20th Street NW, Suite 300, Washington, DC 20036. Phone: 202-296-8400. Website: www.agb.org.

Boardnet USA, a service of the New York Council of Nonprofits, Inc., 272 Broadway, Albany, NY 12204. Phone: 800-515-5012. Website: boardnetusa.org.

BoardSource, 750 9th Street NW, Suite 650, Washington, DC 20001. Phone: 202-349-2580. Website: www.boardsource.org.

CompassPoint Nonprofit Services, 500 12th Street, Suite 320, Oakland, CA 94607. Phone: 510-318-3755. Website: www.compasspoint.org.

Guide Star, 4801 Courthouse Street, Suite 220, Williamsburg, VA 23188. Phone: 757-229-4631. Website: www.guidestar.org.

Independent Sector, 1602 L Street NW, Washington, DC, 20036. Phone: 202-467-6161. Website: www.independentsector.org.

Museum Trustee Association, 211 East Lombard Street, Suite 179, Baltimore, MD 21202. Phone: 410-402-0954. Website: www.museumtrustee.org.

National Council of Nonprofits, 1001 G Street NW, Suite 700 East, Washington, DC 20001. Phone: 202-962-0322. Website: www.councilofnonprofits.org.

Nonprofit Risk Management Center, 204 South King Street, Leesburg, VA 20175. Phone: 703-777-3504. Website: www.nonprofitrisk.org.

About the Museum Trustee Association and the Authors

The Museum Trustee Association was formed as a committee of the American Association of Museums (now known as the American Alliance of Museums) in 1971. Time revealed that the differences of focus, responsibility, and interest between museum professionals and volunteer boards of trustees would be better served by a separate nonprofit organization. The Museum Trustee Association became a separate entity in 1986 and received its federal IRS 501(c)(3) status in 1991. Since then, MTA has been governed by an elected board of directors representing diverse regions of the United States, the Caribbean, Canada, and Mexico, a variety of museum disciplines and sizes, and wide-ranging areas of expertise in trusteeship. All are current or former museum trustees, and several are founders of MTA.

Daryl Fischer founded Musynergy Consulting in 1993 to provide strategic and interpretive planning, audience evaluation, and board development services to museums and other cultural nonprofits. In 2001 she coauthored the first edition of *Building Museum Boards*, followed by *The Leadership Partnership* (2002), *Executive Transitions* (2003), and *Strategic Thinking and Planning* (2004). Her service on numerous nonprofit boards including the Urban Institute for Contemporary Arts (Grand Rapids, Michigan), the Visitor Studies Association, and the Progressive Women's Alliance of the Lakeshore has given her a profound appreciation for the passion, energy, and expertise that board members bring to the organizations they serve. Her consulting practice has taught her that there is no one-size-fits-all formula for maximizing board effectiveness; however, authentic collaboration with staff and community members leads to a whole that is greater than the sum of the parts. Daryl has an MA from the University of Denver and a BA from Colorado College.

Laura B. Roberts is principal of Roberts Consulting, working with cultural nonprofit organizations on strategic planning, assessment, and organizational development. Laura was executive director of the New England Museum Association and the Boston Center for Adult Education. Previously, she was director of education at three history museums. She is the chair of the Central Square Theater in Cambridge, Massachusetts, and formerly chaired the boards of Tufts University Art Gallery, MassHumanities, and First Night Boston. She teaches museum and nonprofit management at Harvard University Extension, Bank Street College of Education, and Northeastern University. Laura holds an MBA from Boston University Questrom School of Business, an MA from the Cooperstown Graduate Program, and a BA from Harvard University.